SKETCH CITY

Tips and Inspiration
for Drawing on Location

DOPRESS BOOKS

CYPI PRESS

FOREWORD

Urban sketching, with its ultimate goal of nothing more than personal enjoyment and recreation, is a hobby to be proud of! It provides us with many delights, including a relaxed and lifted mood, and pleasant experiences. The pleasure lies in the experience of the process, not in the pursuit of perfect work. For urban sketchers, neither expensive tools nor professional artistic training is necessarily required. All they need to do is be prepared to take out their sketchbook in an instant to record exciting anecdotes or plain episodes, whether strolling in strange cities or while standing by familiar roads; these records in the form of sketches will in turn become invaluable and treasured memories.

Reading this book is like getting a glimpse of the artists' sketchbooks. Presented here are hundreds of urban sketch masterpieces from twenty-five artists from all over the world. Most of them are not majors of architectural design, and some even haven't received formal art education. Accordingly, they are less constrained by convention; rather, they show vivid imagination and creativity in their lines, layouts, colors, light, shade, etc., and in their selection and usage of tools and materials which include but are not limited to colored pencils, watercolors, gouache, markers, and coloring software at a later stage. The variety of hand-painting forms and tools also indicates that urban sketching is a kind of free artistic creation, without restrictions of time, space, materials, or tools. Besides showcasing delicate artworks, the artists featured in this book also unreservedly share their creative techniques as well as the personal stories behind each painting with readers.

It is expected that when you finish reading this book, you will be able to pluck up your confidence, take up your pencil and sketchbook, and walk through streets and lanes capturing wonderful moments of the city with heartfelt strokes.

CONTENTS

DRAWING MATERIALS & TECHNIQUES

GLOBAL GALLERY OF URBAN SKETCHERS

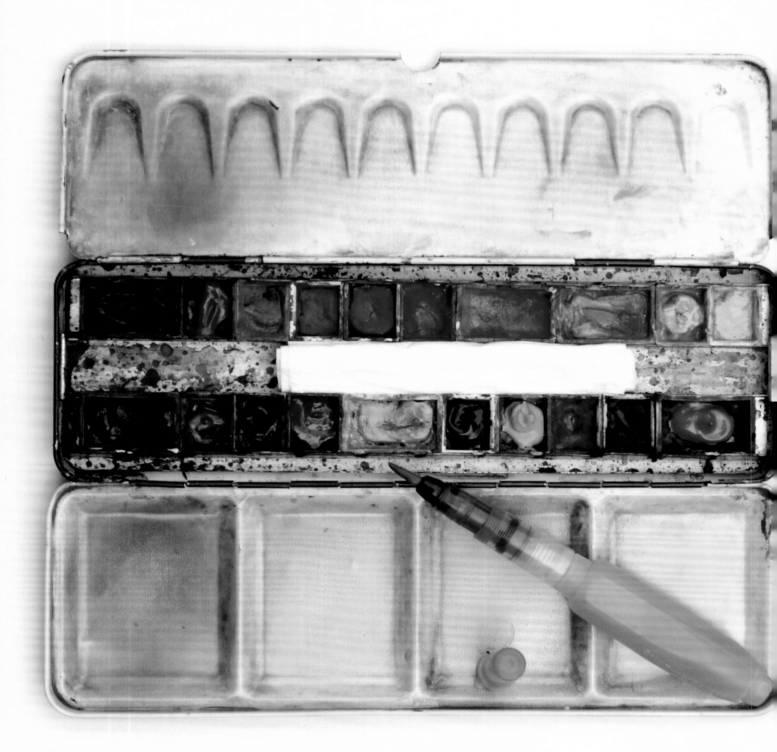

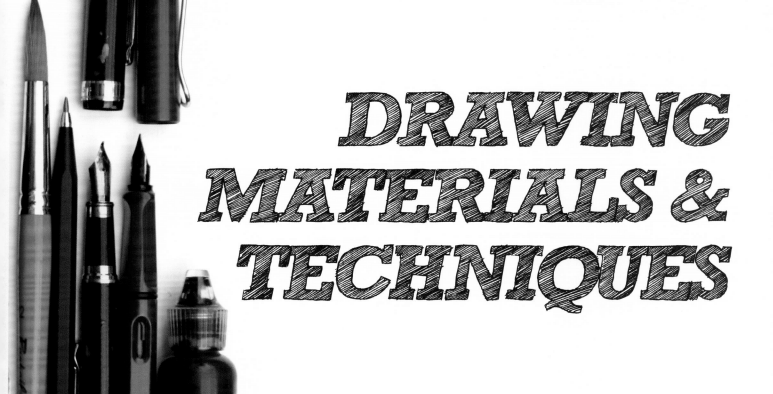

DRAWING MATERIALS & TECHNIQUES

Getting to know sketching

1. What is sketching?

Sketching, as its name suggests, is a method of quick drawing. It resembles outline drawing, which is not just fundamental to formative arts, but also an independent form of art on its own. Sketching was originally the preliminary step and recording method for painters as they began their creation. As this artistic category continued to develop, it later became a compulsory subject for disciplines such as art, design and architecture. Some of the painting masters familiar to us are consummate sketch artists, such as the 17th-century Dutch painter Rembrandt van Rijn, the 18th-century British painter William Hogarth, and the 19th-century German painter Adolph Menzel.

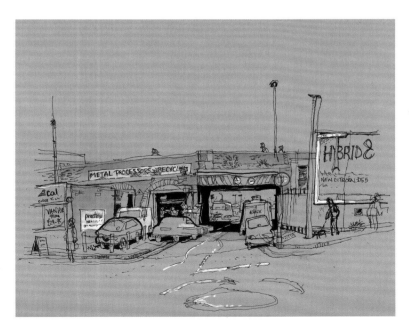

2. Why should we practice sketching?

First, it cultivates sharp perception, which enables us to capture moments of beauty in life. Secondly, it trains our capability of summarization in painting, which prompts us to materialize features of the objects we wish to depict. Thirdly, while a good sketch is itself a perfect piece of art, sketching also helps collect massive amounts of material for our later creations. Fourthly, it boosts our capability of remembering images and writing from memory. For all painters, sketching is the way to perceive life and record feelings. It renders these feelings and images into specific and concrete forms.

3. How to understand urban sketching?

Urban sketching refers to a way of painting in a fast and brief manner that depicts what one views and hears in the city. Objects for its depiction mainly include architecture and cultural landscapes, which gives it another name – urban architecture and landscape sketching. It demonstrates the relationships between architecture, nature, and humanism in the city, as everything in the city operates within these relationships. In urban sketching, they contrast with one another, and each of them requires different methods of depiction. It is suggested that the artist use different lines or techniques so as to differentiate the diversified feelings generated by each of them.

4. Why does sketching remain indispensable even when a digital camera is available?

On the one hand, realistic painting gives prominence to certain elements. In the case when the observer would like to expose inner feelings, a digital camera can hardly reveal the subtlety and concentration that a sketch can. On the other hand, those who favor painting may have different emotions and feelings in creating a landscape painting from photographing the same view – the emotions, techniques and artistic atmosphere embedded in a painting mirror the painter's inner world, which is unachievable with a common digital photograph.

Classification of urban architecture & landscape sketching

1. Forms of expression

Line-oriented sketches

This style is simple and terse. Hard-tipped pens including pencils, pens, and technical pens are suitable for line sketches. The depiction of the objects starts at the structure and conveys the transformations, evolving motions and textures in summarized and simplified lines.

Value-oriented (light and shadow) sketches

This method usually uses thin lines for outlines, followed by brush painting with transition from light colors to darker ones. It depicts shadows with simple blocks and transitions from the background to the foreground.

Line-value combined sketches

This style depicts formative elements such as volume, light and shadow visually, and is suitable for conveying integrated effects of a design and drawing from life. It looks realistic, with enriched layers and vivid expressiveness. This method can depict structural features of objects more than adequately; however it is quite time-consuming, which can be compensated for with bold lines and large blocks for speed.

2. Tools and materials

In terms of tools and materials, sketches can be classified into pencil sketches, pen sketches, water color sketches, charcoal sketches, brush sketches, and so on.

3. Expressive features

Sketches for research and record

These kinds of sketches are usually done by painters or architects while collecting creation materials in research of a certain subject's features, structure, and principles. The goal is to deepen a rational understanding of the subject and get fully prepared for later creation and design. Sketching of this kind can be left unfinished, which means there is no pursuit of completion or perfection of the picture, while emphasis is attached to specific depiction of prominent features of parts of the subject. It can be partial and loose, or converged and integrated; it can take either a long or short time to finish.

Sketches for creation and expression

In sketches created purely for the sake of creation and expression artists entertain their passion for the cities they represent in their work, and endow their pieces with the full display of their expression, desires, and personal emotions to engender the viewer's aesthetic associations. This kind of sketching aims for completion, with priority on vivid portrayals of the atmosphere, layout, effects, and overall momentum in the scene. The final work can be appreciated as a complete picture with independent aesthetic value.

Sketching tools and materials

1. Common tools

Sketching doesn't require particular painting tools. Generally speaking, any tool able to leave a mark on the surface of the material can be used for sketching, such as pencils, fountain pens, ink pens, markers, crayons, technical pens, soft pens, ballpoint pens, carbon pencils, charcoal sticks, painting brushes, watercolor pens, and so on.

The most appealing characteristics of pencils are their convenience, and the ease with which one can adjust their lines and solidity. However, penciled works can be difficult to preserve.

One of the traits of fountain pen paintings is that they are efficient in displaying effects with distinctive prominence and strong contrast. The pen is distinct and clear but also able to achieve mellowness and subtly, and it is easy to both keep an even line thickness and avoid scrubbing the paper. Works in fountain pen are suitable for long-term preservation, but they are not easily modified and demand much more accuracy in line work.

Ink pens, including water ink pens and oil pens, are one of the most popular tools used by sketch artists. There is a wide selection of colors, they are easy to get, and agreeable to all sorts of environments. While water ink pens have no

particular requirements of paper, oil pens are advised for use on thicker paper as they are more penetrating.

Markers are available in bright colors with a certain degree of transparency, and can apply colors directly and vigorously. Their most prominent trait is changeable nibs, which can create either layers upon layers or gracefully extending images. Markers also have alcohol, oil and water varieties. In selection of paper type, it is suggested to consider how piled paper, when used with markers, may vary in effects.

Watercolor pencils are pure, transparent, clear, and natural in color, which makes them "like a breath of fresh air." They are mixed with water and translucent pigments to paint, which makes them unsuitable for larger works. Many a sketch artist likes watercolors for their ability to create the penetrating effects of layer upon layer of one color covering the other, which gives a unique feeling of harmonious mixture.

Crayons do not penetrate; they adhere to the paper. They cannot generate composite colors through piling different colors up repeatedly, yet they are able to create simple artistic effects full of childlike appeal.

Many sketch artists employ charcoal sticks in pursuit of the effect of combined lines and blocks. Charcoal sticks are dark black in color, which makes them appear to be the ultimate simple and real material for sketching. As there is no gel, coarser materials may be painted on charcoal marks using a strong adhesive force to facilitate later modifications.

2. Commonly used paper types

There are multiple paper types for sketching, such as drawing paper, sketch paper, art paper, card paper, bamboo-made paper, rice paper, and so on. Different pens require correspondent paper types. Fountain pens normally agree with smooth and impermeable type of paper, such as card stock and art paper. Pencil sketches are usually drawn on coarse, thick, or rough paper, such as sketch paper, painting paper, and bamboo-made paper. Brush sketches generally go with soft, highly absorbent type of paper, such as rice paper, bamboo-made paper, and so on.

Apart from single piece of paper suitable for drawing, there are all kinds of sketchbooks and booklets available on the market whose main advantages are that they are easy to carry, use, and preserve.

Common problems in urban architecture & landscape sketching

1. How to achieve a composition quickly

A fundamental key to fast composition lies in determining the most appropriate foothold, in accordance with the medium being used, which in turn directly determines how much space the subject will take in the entire layout. For starters, the artist is advised to try various footholds so as to perceive the differences in point of view and understand the varied effects created. It is also important to be mindful of the relationship between the viewpoint and the principles of perspectives. Structures of urban landscapes and changes of light and shadows can be diversified on the drawing paper, which requires the sketcher to apply perspective principles with reference to the viewpoint. Additionally, when applying perspective principles, it is better to presume how viewers may observe the scene, as different viewpoints engender different emotions, understandings and appreciation of the drawing.

2. How to better set the proportion and perspective relationships

The establishment of perspectives is basically an understanding of the proportion of the object observed. Apart from fundamental perspective principles such as one-point, two-point and three-point perspectives, there is the standing position of the artist to be considered for setting the style of the drawing, such as portrayal of the magnitude and style of architecture, the surroundings and the weather, and so on. In depicting magnificent architecture, it is suggested that the sketch artist start from a far point on the paper so as to keep it in proportion. This will enable the artist to capture the image without the deviations resulting from an overly close viewpoint.

3. How to determine the relationships between the primary and the subordinate, the complicate and the simple, the virtual and the real as well as the sparse and the dense

The views in a city are either wide and extensive or bustling and crowded, with no ready, ideal scenes set up for us. Therefore, artists must be sober in selecting (either accepting or rejecting) and borrowing the scenes. It is safe to say that direct copying is not a style cast for sketching. To accept is to take in the elements which are typical, important, beautiful, and closely related to the theme and feelings to be conveyed; to reject means to discard those that are irrelevant, atypical, random, and unseemly. Borrowing scenes refers to the transplant of views in close relation to the theme and serving as effective foils to the original views. Hence, urban sketch artists can successfully present multiple ideal works of art with bold selection of scenes.

Nevertheless, it is to be emphasized that selection and borrowing of scenes must be in compliance with the city's inherent features and in harmony with the overall picture.

4. Some techniques in wielding the pen

Landscape sketching demands that the artist be decisive, accurate, and dexterous in making each stroke. Being decisive refers to the degree of skill in setting up the theme and layout. If thoroughly planned, the artist must be stable and composed accordingly; otherwise, the drawing would be disorganized and disorderly. Being accurate refers to the right positions of the layout, which comprises the structure of the object and the conveyance of the subject. Being dexterous is reflected in the general layout, the selection and summarization of objects, and the diversified use of lines. Here are some techniques in how to wield the pen: first, keep a cheerful mood and stay relaxed in all limbs and joints, which contributes to natural transition of the lines; secondly, do not hesitate or pause in sketching the contours so as to ensure smooth lines; thirdly, be mindful of the drawing strength and take care not to overplay.

5. Some techniques in the combination of pigments

Even professional graphics software cannot display all colors in the world, which makes some hues difficult to blend, such as gold and silver. Commonly used pigments include watercolor, gouache, propylene, markers, and oil colors. The coloring features and characteristics of each ingredient determine the effects that a painting can obtain: thus, it is compulsory to get a thorough knowledge of them before truly getting down to drawing. For instance, light watercolor is unable to cover the background color, which can be more easily achieved by oil colors and gouache. Mineral pigments such as ultramarine, ocher, and terra rossa are prone to cause sediments whether used alone or mixed with other colors. Oil colors' overlaying effects and the thickness caused by impasto resemble the traits of watercolors, which are mellow, dense, and fresh with no hint of getting dirty or gray, no matter how you mix them up. The combination of watercolors and markers is recommended if colors are to be applied to a large area.

Nevertheless, technique-wise, every artist boasts their own unique skills and favorite methods of workmanship, all of which are used for the sole sake of creating ideal urban architectural sketch works.

GLOBAL GALLERY OF URBAN SKETCHERS

Corrado Parrini

Corrado Parrini was born in Aosta, Italy, in 1966, and studied graphic design and illustration at the Scuola del Fumetto (Comics School) in Milan. After graduation he immediately started to collaborate with the largest Italian editorial houses, designing and producing hundreds of book covers. In 1998, he moved to Paris where he could enrich his professional skills while integrating the methods and qualities of the French communication market. Gifted with a fine sensibility, Corrado practices different techniques in order to increase the value of his subjects to the maximum.

IN THE WORK OF THE URBAN SKETCHER, DEEP KNOWLEDGE OF THE PLACE IS A FACTOR OF CONSIDERABLE IMPORTANCE.

🧰 Corrado Parrini's drawing tools and materials

In general, for what concerns the work of the urban sketchers, my choice falls on tools and materials that are simple, easy to handle, and quick to use. For practical reasons bottles of color, big bulky brushes and cans of water or thinners do not fall into my "vanity case." I use calligraphy cartridges, permanent markers, brushes with a cartridge refill or water reservoir. Carnets are generally limited in size for easy transport.

🖌 Tools and materials recommended by Corrado Parrini

- Pen: Sheaffer Calligraphy Viewpoint fountain pen; Faber-Castell-Broadpen 1554 (0.8 mm); Pilot V5 Ball; Koh.I.Noor Office (0.5 mm).
- Brush: Pocket Brush Pentel with cartridge refills; Pentel Aquash (Water Brush) of various tips.

👁 City in my eyes

Lisbon – The appearance of popular and colorful houses and inhabitants are the features of this picturesque city. The decline of some of the buildings, the noise of the historic trams, and the succession of ups and downs complete the scene. Even miradouros are typical places of the Portuguese social life and offer an ideal view for a sketcher's work.

Photography: Corrado Parrini

01. Title: *Rua Almada and Rua Saldanha;* **Place:** *Lisbon, Portugal;* **Duration:** *2 hours;* **Size:** *36 x 28 cm;* **Tools & Materials:** *ink pen on paper and digital color.*

Arriving on foot from the famous Lift da Bica funicular to the miradouro St. Catarina, one meets this small crossroads. Seemingly trivial elements combine to give all the characteristics of the charm of Lisbon. The colorful facades of the houses overlook the narrow streets that intersect in dizzying ups and downs. Noteworthy is the restaurant A Camponesa, which is right at the point on the Rua Marechal Saldanha.

Tips: "In the work of the urban sketcher, the deep knowledge of the place is a factor of considerable importance. The time and the different light conditions can completely transform a local scene. For this particular job, I had to wait a few hours before the direction of the sunlight enhanced the best characteristics."

01

02

02. Title: *Miradouro St. Luzia 2;* **Place:** *Lisbon, Portugal;* **Duration:** *3 hours;* **Size:** *42 x 29 cm;* **Tools & Materials:** *ink pen on paper and digital color*

The Miradouro St. Luzia is worth several drawing sessions. By varying the point of view, the historic districts of Lisbon, the Alfama and the dome of Sao Vicente da Fora can be glimpsed.

Tips: "When I find myself drawing on a trip I want to have a true moment of pleasure and fun. So, I try to find myself in the best conditions of comfort and relaxation, possibly in front of an amazing place; this miradouro definitely focuses all of these qualities. If the work turns into fun you can be sure that you will see the results!"

04

03. *Title:* Miradouro São Pedro; *Place:* Lisbon, Portugal; *Duration:* 3 hours; *Size:* 59 × 21 cm; *Tools & Materials:* ink pen on paper and digital color

The Miradouro of Bairro Alto has a large garden on two terraces and views of the city. A stop on the benches can be a source of inspiration at any time of the day, as well as a beneficial break after all of the inevitable ups and downs a visit to the city imposes. The contrast of colors offered in the hour before sunset is breathtaking.

Tips: "For complex compositions, start by drawing on the sheet, with light strokes, the position of all the important elements, and defined and detailed elements in the foreground; reduce the stroke weight and the amount of details as you move away from the first floor. In this way, the feeling of depth will be enhanced to the maximum."

04. *Title:* Port de l'Arsenal; *Place:* Paris, France; *Duration:* 3 hours; *Size:* 59 × 21 cm; *Tools & Materials:* ink pen on paper and digital color

From the Place de la Bastille the road leads to the Port de l'Arsenal. Nearby there's a perfect place to spend a pleasant break outside of urban traffic and noise. It is a real heaven for tourist boats, some of which have been turned into houses that remain moored full time.

Tips: "This design was made with the same pen as the former work and was then scanned and colored with Photoshop later. I drew as quickly as possible to translate the stretch vibration of color and light on the contours."

05

05. *Title: The Beach Barceloneta; Place: Barcelona, Spain; Duration: 3 hours; Size: 59 × 21 cm; Tools & Materials: ink pen on paper and digital color*

The Barcelona's beach is totally artificial, so it does not shine with a natural and wild charm. It remains an important venue in the city's social life. Almost five kilometres long, the area is home to a multitude of restaurants and kiosks that offer catering, as well as countless live concerts and parties until late at night. The walk along the Passeig del Mare Nostrum is very pleasant and full of ideas.

Tips: "We should not try to describe it all, for too many details confuse the viewer and make heavy work. Essential features side by side with elements less detailed or or even left 'fuzzy' accentuate the depth and life of the scene as well as suggest movement."

06. *Title: Barceloneta Seen from the Harbor; Place: Barcelona, Spain; Duration: 1.5 hours; Size: 59 × 21 cm; Tools & Materials: ink pen and water on paper*

The old port of Barcelona occupies a large and important area where design structures and modern constructions have been joined to the ancient buildings that bear witness to the splendor of the maritime tradition of the Catalan capital. From a comfortable bench just around the aquarium the artist viewed this picturesque corner of the dock.

Tips: "For the execution of this design, I used a simple Tratto pen. This is the famous felt-tip marker by FILA, an Italian manufacturing compay. It can be diluted with water. Just draw the outlines of the figures, then brush with water – it will dissolve the ink, creating halftones."

07. *Title: Barrio Alto Rua; Place: Lisbon, Portugal; Duration: 1.5 hours; Size: 50 × 21 cm; Tools & Materials: ink pen on paper and watercolors*

Often, during a move from one tourist spot to another the best framings can be found. Its low and colorful houses with small private gardens and the calm, shady alleys of this particular corner of the Bairro Alto made the artist completely forget his initial destination...

Tips: "In these perfect conditions I could fully enjoy the luxury of a classic coloring in watercolor. With the addition of water, even the ink tract melts and softens the contours and atmosphere."

09

08. *Title:* Quai de Seine (Pont de Tolbiac); *Place:* Paris, France; *Duration:* 3 hours; *Size:* 59 × 21 cm; *Tools & Materials:* ink pen and digital color

The Seine and its banks have always inspired artists of all ages. In summer, the riverbanks offer a perfect place – fresh and easy to access, where you can find endless scenarios and picturesque views. It's interesting that the industrial facilities directly related to the transport of aggregates still takes place via barges on the great river to the sea.

Tips: "In this case I chose a landscape away from the usual tourist clichés. The stretch of river in question is located near the Tolbiac Bridge in the 13th arrondissement."

09. *Title:* Place de la Bastille; *Place:* Paris, France; *Duration:* 50 minutes; *Size:* 59 × 21 cm; *Tools & Materials:* ink pen on paper

This important Parisian square is the hub of traffic and socio-cultural life of the ville lumière (City of Light). The square, in the middle of a downtown entertainment district and major cultural event center, is a privileged place for the observation of city life at all hours of the day and night.

Tips: "My point of view is a convenient bench on the vast terrace between the Opera Bastille and the Boulevard Bourdon."

10. *Title:* Miradouro St. Luzia; *Place:* Lisbon, Portugal; *Duration:* 3 hours; *Size:* 42 × 29 cm; *Tools & Materials:* ink pen on paper and digital color

The drawing shows the view from the terrace of the small miradouro Santa Luzia looking toward the river Tejo. The sun sets behind and slowly the shadow overtakes the roofs of the houses below, creating a captivating game of contrasts.

Tips: "The sun goes down quickly and we can not afford to meditate too much on the beauty of the landscape. When you portray places of great tourist interest and, therefore, high attendance, it is crucial to find an observation area where you are sure that the comings and goings of tourists does not obstruct your view continuously."

Febvre Georges

Febvre Georges worked as a dental surgeon up to 2013. After ten years of nude life model drawing, he started sketching in 2010, attending a one-year sketching class by Nicolas Doucedame at "The Académie Libre" (Free Academy) in Aix-en-Provence, France. Since 2012, he has been organizing monthly sketching Saturdays with other aficionados, all around Aix, just to share this pleasant activity with like-minded friends. For more information, please visit his websites: www.flickr.com/photos/constantigeorges/; aixcroquis.over-blog.net; georgesfebvre.over-blog.com.

🧰 Febvre Georges' drawing tools and materials

I'm fond of improvising and trying new tools. I also take inspiration from other artists' works. I tend to start with a pen; with more complex subjects, a light pencil sketch helps me a lot.

✏ Tools and materials recommended by Febvre Georges

- Mechanical pencil 0.5 mm; Elastomer eraser, Tombow Mono Zero 2.3 mm.
- Stylo Hero M86, Noodler's black ink (bulletproof).
- Platinum Carbon pen, and ink cartridge carbon black.
- Faber Castell glass fibre eraser pen.
- Escoda Kolinsky – Tajmyr sable retractable round watercolor Brushes n°6 – 10.
- Watercolors Horadam de Schmincke (transparent orange), Watercolors Daler Rowney (cerulean blue), Moleskine sketchbooks.

Photography: Andrea Schaffer

👁 City in my eyes

Aix-en-Provence is a beautiful city in the south of France. One of several of the city's world-famous sites, Cours Mirabeau attracts visitors from local areas and abroad. It is a wide thoroughfare planted with double rows of plane trees, bordered by fine houses, and decorated with fountains. Aix-en-Provence is also well known for artist Paul Cezanne, who was born there and painted many views of The Sainte Victoire Mountain.

01

02

> BE PATIENT AND CONSTRUCTIVE AT THE BEGINNING, AND THE REWARDS WILL COME LATER.

01. *Title:* Le Miroir aux Oiseaux: Ornamental Bird-Pond; *Place:* Martigues, France; *Duration:* 4 hours; *Size:* 60 x 22 cm; *Tools & Materials:* fountain pen Lamy EF nib, ink platinum carbon black water-resist, drawing gum, Winsor & Newton watercolors and sketchbook Vang 30 × 21 cm, 230 gr/m²

Nicknamed Venice of Provence, Martigues is a point of passage between the Mediterranean Sea and the étang de Berre. This place is called the bird mirror because formerly the walls of the channel were covered with bushes, making it a paradise for birds, which were reflected in the water. As always, classical drawing at first and then watercolor splashes with color vibration.

Tips: "I started with a light pencil drawing of the main perspective lines; then, I drew with the water-resistant ink before using watercolors. Afterwards, I used the drawing gum for the calligraphy, the left trees, and the street lamps. The watercolor splashes in the sky were then possible."

02. *Title:* Saint Sauveur Cathedral, Aix; *Place:* Aix-en-Provence, France; *Duration:* 4 hours; *Size:* 60 × 22 cm; *Tools & Materials:* Rohrer & Klingner glass dip pen, Rohrers & Klingner Ausziehtusche bister ink, Winsor & Newton watercolors, Pilot Choose 07 white and sketchbook Vang 30 x 21 cm, 230 gr/m²

Aix Cathedral is a Roman Catholic cathedral. It is built on the site of the first-century Roman forum of Aix. It is a national monument of France. After starting sketching the architecture in a classical way, the artist decided to change and to finish with watercolors, loosely, in a non-conventional way, with run-off.

Tips: "I really appreciate perspective line distortions. As the cathedral was a serious subject, I decided to be less graphic and looser in the use of watercolor. The tree was too green… I improved it by adding white doodles done with the Pilot Choose 07."

27

03. *Title: La Place des Quatre Dauphins; **Place:** Aix-en-Provence, France; **Duration:** 3 hours; **Size:** 30 × 21 cm; **Tools & Materials:** pencil HB and Winsor & Newton watercolors and Clairefontaine watercolor sketchbook 30 x 21cm*

The Fountain des Quatre Dauphins is situated in the center of the square with the same name, in the Quartier Mazarin, not far from the Cours Mirabeau. Five days after this watercolor was finished, the plane tree on the right fell down during a big storm. In this example, the observer can see strong light, typical of Provence.

Tips: "Shade and light are important… Avoid color uniformity in shade (such as always blue). You have to mix warm and cold colors so that you get warm and cold shades."

04. *Title: Fuveau Railway Station; **Place:** Fuveau, France; **Duration:** 3 hours; **Size:** 30 x 21 cm; **Tools & Materials:** Hero M86 fountain pen, Noodler's black bulletproof, Winsor & Newton watercolors and Clairefontaine sketchbook 30 x 21 cm*

In Cézanne's country, some enthusiasts bring the trains of yesteryear back to life for the pleasure of young and old alike; these volunteers also manage the Provencal Museum of Transports and can organize friendly visits. Fuveau is situated near Gardanne, which was formerly the heart of the coal-mining area of Provence.

Tips: "It is important to establish a realistic perspective so that you can be more creative in the use of watercolors; be patient and constructive at the beginning, and the rewards will come later. Don't draw the whole page… Don't tell the whole story."

05. *Title: Darius Milhaud Music Conservatory; **Place:** Aix-en-Provence, France; **Duration:** 4 hours; **Size:** 60 × 22 cm; **Tools & Materials:** Lamy fountain pen, EF nib, ink platinum carbon black water-resist, stylo pilot parallel pen 6.0 and 3.8 mm, Winsor & Newton watercolors and Vang sketchbook 30 x 21 cm, 230 gr/m²*

Designed by Kengo Kuma, the new conservatory of Aix-en-Provence is a type of rhythmic monolith with angles of wood and metal that evoke Japanese origami. An area of 7,000 m² of this space is dedicated to teaching music, dance, and theatre. The artist wanted to transmit the light and contrast of this view.

Tips: "Water-resistant ink is necessary before a watercolor wash, so there will be no color bleeding. Pilot parallel pens are easy to use but the ink isn't water-resistant, so use them at the very end of your sketch."

06. *Title: Le Corbusier's Cité Radieuse; **Place:** Marseille, France; **Duration:** 4 hours; **Size:** 60 × 22 cm; **Tools & Materials:** Lamy fountain pen, EF nib, ink platinum carbon black water-resist, drawing gum, Winsor & Newton watercolors and Vang sketchbook 30 x 21 cm, 230 gr/m²*

Le Corbusier (1887-1965) built La Cité Radieuse between 1947 and 1952. The flat roof is designed as a communal terrace with sculptural ventilation stacks, a running track, and a shallow paddling pool for children. There is also a children's art school in the workshop. The roof has unobstructed views of the Mediterranean Sea and Marseille, and can be accessed by the public.

Tips: "By adding figures to your sketch, your feeling of depth will be enhanced. Apply abundant water on the paper so that you can see flows afterwards by titling your sketchbook. A Hero fountain pen is very useful because it can change the width of your lines."

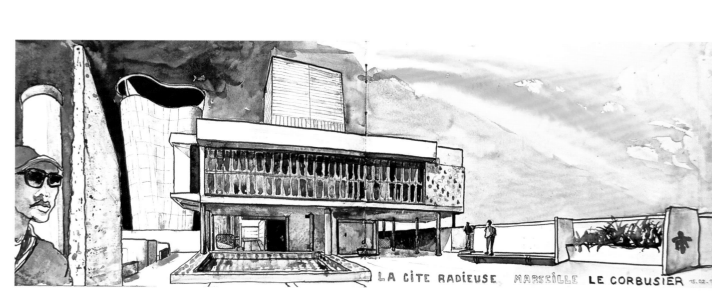

06

07. *Title:* La Madeleine; *Place:* Aix-en-Provence, France; *Duration:* 3 hours; *Size:* 30 × 21 cm; *Tools & Materials:* pencil drawing and Winsor & Newton watercolors and Clairefontaine sketchbook 30 × 21 cm

The Madeleine church is a religious building in the Moralizers' square in Aix-en-Provence. This square owes its name to a Dominican convent on the foundations of which the Sainte Madeleine church was built from 1691 to 1703 by the architect Laurent Vallon. It was considered for a long time as the most beautiful religious building in this part of Provence. Splashes and runs of watercolors reach beyond the original purpose.

Tips: "With watercolors, use only few colors; in this case, Indian yellow, cerulean blue and French ultramarine blue were used. Liquid flows and splashes are always distracting and attractive."

08. *Title:* Gardanne; *Place:* Gardanne, France; *Duration:* 3 hours; *Size:* 41 × 12.5 cm; *Tools & Materials:* Sennelier inks and pen (Chinese black and sanguine) and Moleskine watercolor sketchbook 21 x 13 cm

Gardanne is a small town between Aix-en-Provence and Marseille. A railway was built in the 1860s and the mines were dug a little later, attracting Italian, Armenian, Polish, Czech, Spanish, and African workers to the village. The deep mine, one of the last surviving in France, was closed down in 2003. On the left, it's the only view of the village ever painted by Cézanne.

Tips: "Through the windshield of my car, every day of my working life, I saw this impressive industrial structure, owned by an aluminum manufacturer. I wanted to mix the red of the bauxite supply and the black of this coal mine city; take the time to make sure that all the lines you draw are in contact with the others… no empty space."

08

07

grille de l'hôtel
de ville ~ 17e s.

Aix en Pce

09. *Title:* Grille de L'Hotel de Ville d'Aix-en-Provence; *Place:* Aix-en-Provence, France; *Duration:* 4 hours; *Size:* 60 × 22 cm; *Tools & Materials: fountain pen hero M86, ink Noodlers black, Rohrer & Klingner glass dip pen, brushes, Sennelier ink and Vang sketchbook 30 x 21 cm, 230 gr/m²*

The magnificent city hall of Aix-en-Provence dominates one of the most beautiful squares in the city. Pierre Pavillon built it in the middle of the 17th century; it is characterized by its magnificent wrought iron railing and its main staircase. This red brown ink corresponds exactly to the color of the massive entrance gate decorated with lionhead knockers.

Tips: "When you use a sketchbook, it's better to start in the middle of the two pages although it can be frightening… You'll be sure to have a link between the two pages."

eglise
st laurent

marseille

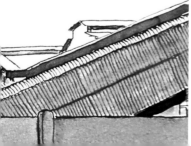

10. *Title:* Saint Laurent Church; *Place:* Martigues, France; *Duration:* 3 hours; *Size:* 60 × 22 cm; *Tools & Materials: fountain pen hero M86, Noodlers black ink, Rohrer and Klingner glass dip pen, brushes, Sennelier ink and Vang sketchbook 30 x 21 cm, 230 gr/m²*

Implanted on the mound Saint Laurent, called today "La Tourette," this church had to be near the castle Babon. Searches and excavations done nearby showed the existence of a Greek housing environment from the beginning of the foundation of the Phoenician city. The artist has stressed deliberately the perspective so that everything goes into the panoramic size of the frame. The watercolor was thrown to obtain an attractive dynamic effect.

Tips: "I enjoy mixing a precise realistic drawing with free-loose splashes of watercolor; you have to apply abundant clear water on your pages before using the watercolor. When stressing perspectives, I like the strength of Chinese ink applied with a glass dip pen. Some calligraphy close to the subject does well in this case."

Angelo Rodrigues

Angelo Rodrigues was born in the city of Rio de Janeiro. He graduated in Actuarial Science and taught Actuarial Risk Management in some universities for many years. His artistic foundation was laid in the Parque Lage School of Visual Arts in the early 80s. There he specialized in watercolor, drawing, and metal and wood engraving. Angelo remains permanently tuned to the architecture of the city where he lives, registering his view in urban sketches.

🧰 Angelo Rodrigues' drawing tools and materials

I generally use the Hero M86 pen, Lamy Safari fine nib pen and Lamy mechanical pencil with the 0.5 mm 2B graphite. I use many types of sketchbooks. I make some myself with leftover paper from my wood engraving and metal prints. I also use Moleskine sketchbooks for watercolor and some other sketchbooks that I find here in Brazil.

✒ Tools and materials recommended by Angelo Rodrigues

• Watercolor Graphite (pans) made by ARTGRAF in Portugal creates a watercolor graphite with great luster and delicacy.
• Watercolor Sketching book – the sketching books produced by Atlantis Art Materials and The Langton Prestige Daler Rowney notebooks. These receive the watercolor well and allow for a good control over the colors.
• Pen – Lamy Safari for the practicality and the flowing strokes. Hero M86 pen (calligraphic) offers great creative possibilities with its intense but delicate lines.
• Watercolor Paint: I really enjoy the Sketcher's Pocket Box from Windsor & Newton. The compact case holds up to twelve colors and is practical to use while working outdoors.
• Ink for pen: I always use the Bulletproof Noodler's Ink because they do not mix with the watercolor that is painted over afterwards.

• Brush: I really enjoy the Pentel Arts Aquash brushes because they make it easier to sketch using watercolor.

👁 City in my eyes

I live in Rio de Janeiro and in terms of natural beauty everything around here is exuberant. Our architecture is extremely eclectic, ranging from the 18th-century style up to the Oscar Niemeyer projects. I prefer to focus my work on buildings connected to daily life of people. I find it fascinating how barbershops, bars, restaurants and street markets tell us the stories of the interaction between people.

Photography: Angelo Rodrigues

01

SOMETIMES THE STORY OF A
PLACE CAN MOTIVATE YOUR
SKETCH.

"

01. *Title:* Ladeira dos Tabajaras; **Place:** Rio de Janeiro, Brazil; **Duration:** 1.5 hours; **Size:** 27.5 × 21 cm; **Tools & Materials:** Hero M86 pen with bulletproof ink black and watercolor on Tilibra sketchbook

Ladeira dos Tabajaras (something like Tabajaras' Slope), Copacabana. Tabajara is the name of a native Brazilian tribe. In Tupi language Tabajara means "Lord of our village." The central building is a very old bar, frequented by workers living the region. The motorcycle taxi represented in the picture take residents to the highest parts of the hill.

Tips: "In this image, I found the hanging garden to be the focal point of the scene. Sometimes focusing your energy on the focal point will give you a good result."

02

03

02. **Title:** *Parque Lage Stables;* **Place:** *Rio de Janeiro, Brazil;* **Duration:** *2 hours;* **Size:** *41 × 13 cm;* **Tools & Materials:** *fine black marker on Moleskine watercolor*
Located in Parque Lage, this building is still known as "The Stables," because it used to be the stables of the Lage family, the former owners of the place. Parque Lage is a public park in the city of Rio de Janeiro, located in the Botanical Garden, a neighborhood at the Corcovado Mountain.

Tips: "A building that was built at the beginning of the 20th century to serve as a stable, now houses an art school. Sometimes the story of a place can motivate your sketch."

03. **Title:** *Batman Alley;* **Place:** *São Paulo, Brazil;* **Duration:** *3 hours;* **Size:** *25.4 × 17.8 cm;* **Tools & Materials:** *color marker, Hero pen and watercolor*
This drawing was done in Batman's Alley, an area in São Paulo known for a ubiquitous presence of graffiti. The objective of this piece is to register the interaction between some of the beautiful graffiti with the surroundings.

Tips: "A sketch like any other work of art does not have to compromise with reality. Look for a color composition that works for your art, but does not necessarily represent the reality."

04. *Title:* BB Cultural Centre; *Place:* São Paulo, Brazil; *Duration:* 4 hours; *Size:* 21 × 29.5 cm; *Tools & Materials: Liquid watercolor applied with a brush and fountain pen in a Daler-Rowney sketchbook (150 g/m² – Acid Free Cartridge Paper)*

This is a drawing of the Cultural Centre of the Bank of Brazil in São Paulo. It shows the constrast in the central region of the city between classic architecture and the ever growing presence of modern buildings.

Tips: "In certain moments the architecture is only a reason for you to experiment with colors. Try to make good use of the watercolor in the construction of your sketches."

05. *Title:* Batman Alley – Mural Graffiti; *Place:* São Paulo, Brazil; *Duration:* 2.5 hours; *Size:* 14.5 × 9 cm; *Tools & Materials: Moleskine watercolor, watercolor and pencil*

This drawing seeks to display with some detail a huge panel made by just one street artist. It evokes the roots of contemporary muralism.

Tips: "When drawing graffiti, do not try to make an accurate representation of the street art. Focus on showing their relation with the environment."

04

05

06. *Title:* Amarelinho; *Place:* Rio de Janeiro, Brazil; *Duration:* 2.5 hours; *Size:* 21 × 27.5 cm; *Tools & Materials:* Lamy Safari pen fine nib with bulletproof ink black and watercolor on Tilibra sketchbook

The name of the building is Amarelinho (something like Yellowish), located in Cinelândia. The place is a bohemian area of Rio de Janeiro. There are bars, restaurants, cinemas, theaters and local music. It is a wonderfull place to visit during the night.

Tips: "When you are sketching in a crowded place, try to capture the chaotic nature of the scene."

07. *Title:* Batman Alley – Dancing Bar; *Place:* São Paulo, Brazil; *Duration:* 2 hours; *Size:* 27.5 × 21 cm; *Tools & Materials:* Lamy Fountain pen Safari with black bulletproof ink and watercolor on Tilibra sketchbook

Batman's Alley is made of a group of narrow streets in Vila Madalena, São Paulo. Graffiti artists have covered many surfaces with their art. Those interested in this type of art will probably enjoy visiting the place.

Tips: "When looking for a subject for your sketch, be on the lookout for unique and interesting architectural 'accidents' such as this."

07

08. Title: *Primeiro de Março Street;* **Place:** *Rio de Janeiro, Brazil;* **Duration:** *3 hours;* **Size:** *27.5 × 21 cm;* **Tools & Materials:** *Hero M86 pen, Lamy Safari Fine Nib with bulletproof black ink and watercolor on Tilibra sketchbook*

Rua Primeiro de Março (something like the 1st of March Street), formerly known as Rua Direita, is the oldest street in Rio de Janeiro and was the most important street during the 19th century. In 1875, it was renamed the 1st of March Street in celebration of the allied victory of the Battle of Aquidabã, which put an end to the Paraguai war. Coincidentally, this is also the foundation for the city of Rio de Janeiro.

Tips: "Sometimes the thematic contrast can be the main interest of your image. In this case presenting these 19th-century buildings next to the chaotic traffic of a modern city creates this powerful contrast."

09. Title: *Copacabana at Night;* **Place:** *Rio de Janeiro, Brazil;* **Duration:** *2 hours;* **Size:** *28 × 19 cm;* **Tools & Materials:** *watercolor and Hero pen; Bockingford Economical Thick watercolor Pad 300 GSM – NOT SURFACE (by Atlantis Art Materials-UK)*

This drawing shows one of the few remaining small buildings still existent in Copacabana. This building holds a group of stores and restaurants frequented by locals and tourists.

Tips: "When you are sketching a somewhat decadent building, try to capture the diversity of images that it offers."

Isa Fischer

Isa Fischer holds a university degree in Graphic Design. She has worked as a freelance graphic designer ever since finishing school, focusing mainly on illustration. A sketchbook accompanies her on every journey she takes and she is always portraying her surroundings. In 2013 it occurred to Isa that she should sketch 100 houses in Bremen, her home city, which she then proceeded to do. By the end of that year she had drawn nearly 200 buildings and houses.

> " A SKETCHBOOK ACCOMPANIES HER ON EVERY JOURNEY SHE TAKES! "

🧰 Isa Fischer's drawing tools and materials

You can determine that I'm going sketching because of the large, flat shoulder bag I'm carrying. It contains my aquarelle pad. There's another bag to bring along quills, brushes, ink and aquarelle colors. I usually look for places to sit down that are close to what I am about to draw, such as steps.

✏ Tools and materials recommended by Isa Fischer

• Black ink Pelikan (Scribtol): This ink is very black and opaque; it works fine with a drawing pen.
• Horadam watercolor from Schmincke. Bright colors. Spread excellently.
• HIRO Leonardt nibs, drawing pen, medium soft, blank. These pen nibs do not hurt the paper and the ink flows reliably.
• ISABEY Kolinsky watercolor brush, size 6 well suited to water-colors of ink drawings.
• Kolinsky red sable watercolor brush da Vinci Series 36 of the finest Kolinsky red sable hair.

👁 City in my eyes

Bremen is a city in northern Germany located next to the River Weser, whose historic old quarter offers numerous renaissance facades. What's special about Bremen is that it has an inner-city harbor where crops, coffee and fish meal have been handled for as long as you can remember. The harbor is where historic industrial buildings mix with modern architecture.

Photography: Isa Fischer

01

01. *Title:* Steintor, Bremen; *Place:* Bremen, Germany; *Duration:* 1.5 hours; *Size:* 21 × 24 cm; *Tools & Materials:* ink and watercolor
The sketch shows the varied and colorful architecture of the bohemian side of Bremen.

Tips: "The ink sketch shows roughly the outlines of houses and shops. The colors were loosely dabbed using a brush. It is important not to forget unimportant details, such as road signs and cables to make the sketch authentic."

02. *Title:* *Town Center Bremen;* ***Place:*** *Town Center, Bremen;* ***Duration:*** *2 hours;* ***Size:*** *32 × 45 cm;* ***Tools & Materials:*** *ink and watercolor*
The tram is typical public transport of Bremen.

Tips: "First, I drew the outlines of the houses and trees in broad strokes. When I was drawing the watercolor painting, some parts of the sheet were saved. Thus, the drawing remains looser."

03. *Title:* *Marktplatz;* ***Place:*** *Bremen, Germany;* ***Duration:*** *3 hours;* ***Size:*** *32 × 45 cm;* ***Tools & Materials:*** *ink and watercolor*
For this job the artist was booked by a nice woman from India who loves to sit in the old city centre with her sister when she is visiting. Because it was very cold in Bremen on the day of drawing, the artist asked permission to sit at the window of the first floor of a conveniently located national bank. Permission was promptly given, so the artist was warm enough to draw the picture.

Tips: "The buildings have a lot of architectural details. In contrast, the space in the foreground is drawn bright and easy. A few passers-by show the difference in size of the buildings."

04

05

04. *Title:* *Korsett Friedel;* ***Place:*** *Bremen, Germany;* ***Duration:*** *3.5 hours;* ***Size:*** *32 × 45 cm;* ***Tools & Materials:*** *ink and watercolor*

This is a beautiful shop for ladies' lingerie, where it seems that every single woman in Bremen buys her bras. The artist sat across the road in a café and had several coffees while drawing.

Tips: "It is good to consider in advance how many colors I want to use. The house is decorated in various shades of green to keep the shops colorful and animated."

05. *Title:* *Gendarmenplatz;* ***Place:*** *Berlin, Germany;* ***Duration:*** *2 hours;* ***Size:*** *32 × 45 cm;* ***Tools & Materials:*** *ink and watercolor*

The Gendarmenmarkt is a square in the historic center of Berlin. It is flanked on the north side by the French cathedral.

Tips: "The building is drawn from the bottom. This means that you have to pay attention to the reductions to show the proper perspective."

06. *Title:* *Historic Center;* ***Place:*** *Bremen, Germany;* ***Duration:*** *4 hours;* ***Size:*** *32 × 45 cm;* ***Tools & Materials:*** *ink and watercolor*

A friend of the artist who has his office in the old historic center of Bremen let her sit on his roof-deck for this picture. She had to come twice since it began to rain the first time.

Tips: "Drawing this set of nested houses forced me to concentrate seriously. Since the perspective is from above the rooftops, it is important to pay close attention to the foreshortening."

06

07

07. *Title:* *Hohentorshafen;* ***Place:*** *Bremen, Germany;* ***Duration:*** *1 hour;* ***Size:*** *42 × 15 cm;* ***Tools & Materials:*** *ink and watercolor*

The River Weser flows through Bremen. The bridge depicted in the background is only for trains and one can see the steeple of the Stephani-Church.

Tips: "The sketch was made with bold black strokes of the pen. It is important to look closely at the many details to put them in the correct proportion to each other."

08. *Title:* *Isestraße;* ***Place:*** *Hamburg, Germany;* ***Duration:*** *1.5 hours;* ***Size:*** *21 × 24 cm;* ***Tools & Materials:*** *ink and watercolor*

The artist captured the spring-like atmosphere on a Saturday afternoon in one of Hamburg's busy avenues.

Tips: "The pen and ink drawing shows only at the center of the drawing exactly how the bridge and the houses look like. To the sides the watercolor paint leads a life of its own, which makes the drawing lively and interesting."

09. *Title:* *Harbor of Bremen;* ***Place:*** *Bremen, Germany;* ***Duration:*** *3.5 hours;* ***Size:*** *32 × 145 cm;* ***Tools & Materials:*** *ink and watercolor*

It is a very nice sunny day at the harbor of Bremen. The artist was lucky to find such a large ship there, as work for such large ships has become scarce.

Tips: "I used a drawing pen and black ink to compose the screen layout. Then I applied the watercolor paint in several layers. I let it dry a few points and then renewed the application of paint to achieve a greater depth."

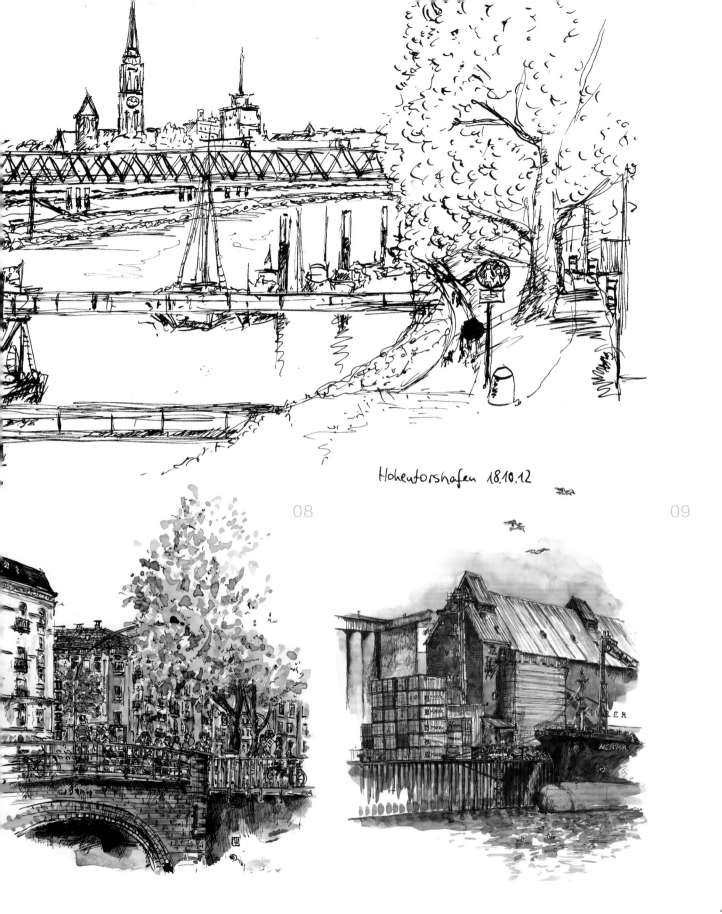

Hohentorshafen 18.10.12

08

09

45

11

12

10. *Title: Power Station; Place: Bremen, Germany; Duration: 3.5 hours; Size: 32 × 45 cm; Tools & Materials: ink and watercolor*

For a good view of this building the artist had to climb on the roof of an office block. The concierge was very friendly and gave her the key for the last door. It is very high and the artist had a wonderful view over the city.

Tips: "It's good to pay attention to a tension-filled layout of the sheet. The tallest building on the left stand alone on the white surface. Towards the right end the drawing focuses attention on the small-scale blue crane."

11. *Title: Stadtmusikanten; Place: Bremen, Germany; Duration: 2 hours; Size: 32 × 45 cm; Tools & Materials: ink and watercolor*

Bremen's most famous landmark is the Town Musicians of Bremen, known to children and adults alike all over the world. Many tourists have their photographs taken with them. A sketch is better...

Tips: "The center of the drawing is the sculpture. The watercolor paint takes it off from the background."

12. *Title: Pollonia; Place: Milos, Greece; Duration: 2 hours; Size: 32 × 45 cm; Tools & Materials: ink and watercolor*

This house is owned by a friend of the artist, who rents it as studios and apartments. Isa stays here whenever she visits the beautiful island of Milos. It's a magical place at the top of a hill where the ocean seems to stretch out in every direction.

Tips: "The house and the steps in the foreground are outlined with black ink. Although the house was left open and mainly green plants have worked out in the drawing, the house is the most important part of the image."

Wim van de Wege

Wim van de Wege was born in 1966. He first studied organ and piano at the Brabants Conservatorium, then visual and fine arts at the Willem de Kooning Academy in Rotterdam. Last year he chose the province of Zeeland as his main creative theme. He shows various landscapes in grand ways, and the characteristic scenery of Zeeland can be found in every one of his works. He prefers to work in the open air with watercolor and pen.

🧰 Wim van de Wege's drawing tools and materials

I am often very busy with sketching and this technique, with watercolor and pen, is a great fit for me. I love the smooth, spontaneous drawing style, in which the elements are fixed in time with ink color. I also create a lot of acrylic landscape paintings for I do prefer to work in the open air. I work with paper, carton, canvas and all that is paintable.

✏ Tools and materials recommended by Wim van de Wege

- Watercolor: Rembrandt, the beautiful mix of the colors.
- Pen: Lettraset, which signs just fine.
- Acrylic: Rembrandt, good spread-ability, beautiful pigments.
- Sketchbook: Moleskine, quality heavy paper and perfect for sketches.
- Watercolor brushes: Pro Arte, making the best brush around.

👁 City in my eyes

In recent years I have drawn about 140 drawings in Dutch cities and towns. Most cities have a history, and I would like to show it in my work. Every year I make several trips to admire foreign cities and draw them out. This is again a great experience for me every time.

ALLOW ONLY ESSENTIAL DETAILS. THE SUGGESTION IS AS IMPORTANT AS THE DETAIL.

Photography: Wim van de Wege

01

01. *Title: Veere Old City; Place: Middelburg, the Netherlands; Duration: 45 minutes; Size: 25 × 25 cm; Tools & Materials: pen and watercolor on paper*

Veere is a beautiful city with a glorious past. It is one of the most surprising locations in Zeeland. In the 17th and 18th centuries, Veere was a prosperous trading city with about 750 houses inside the city walls, compared to about 300 as of 2013.

Tips: "The city hall and the trees are a perfect vanishing point."

02. *Title:* Yerseke Harbor in the Evening; *Place:* Yerseke, the Netherlands; *Duration:* 3 hours; *Size:* 30 × 20 cm; *Tools & Materials:* pen and watercolor
The fishing village is well known for its aquaculture. Oyster boats and most of Europe's mussel vessels sail out from the harbor every day. The artist sketched it to show his love for the place.

Tips: "The horizon is at one third from the top. The water provides forms for space."

02

03

03. *Title:* Kloetinge with the Geerteschurch; *Place:* Kloetinge, the Netherlands; *Duration:* 3 hours; *Size:* 25 × 25 cm; *Tools & Materials:* pen and watercolor
This lovely village lies east of Goes. At its centre is a Gothic church. The "Geertekerk" church breathes the atmosphere of times long gone.

Tips: "This drawing shows the wall on the left, giving extra depth to the image."

04. *Title:* Middelburg Damplein; *Place:* Middelburg, the Netherlands; *Duration:* 3 hours; *Size:* 20 × 30 cm; *Tools & Materials:* pen and watercolor on paper
Around this square are beautiful mansions. In the background is the Lange Jan high abbey tower, which was built in the 17th century.

Tips: "Allow only essential details. The suggestion is as important as the detail."

04

Middelburg januari 2014

05. *Title: Kloetinge Windmill; Place: Kloetinge, the Netherlands; Duration: 3 hours; Size: 25 × 25 cm; Tools & Materials: pen and watercolor*
There are many windmills in the Netherlands. The mill Kloetinge is a round brick tower built in 1704. In Zeeland tradition, it is whitewashed.

Tips: "The white mill has only one color on one side; the other side is suggestion."

06. *Title: Oudelande, a Little Village in de Zak van Zuid-Beveland; Place: Oudelande, the Netherlands; Duration: 3 hours; Size: 25 × 25 cm; Tools & Materials: pen and watercolor*
De Zak van Zuid-Beveland is a natural wonderland in Zeeland. There are many picturesque villages, including Oudelande.

Tips: "Light and shade give the drawing additional expression."

05

06

07

08

07. **Title:** *Kattendijke, a Small Village;* **Place:** *Kattendijke, the Netherlands;* **Duration:** *3 hours;* **Size:** *30 × 20 cm;* **Tools & Materials:** *pen and watercolor*
Kattendijke is a small village that lies on the Oosterschelde.

Tips: "The autumn colors yellow, sienne and green create a moody effect."

08. **Title:** *Ellewoutsdijk Marina;* **Place:** *Ellewoutsdijk, the Netherlands;* **Duration:** *3 hours;* **Size:** *30 × 20 cm;* **Tools & Materials:** *watercolor and pen on paper*
Ellewoutsdijk is located on the Westerschelde and has a little marina. It is gloomy, but the sailing boats make for a nice composition.

Tips: "Red makes for a nice contrast to the blue."

09. Title: *Middelburg Oostkerk;*
Place: *Middelburg, the Netherlands;*
Duration: *3 hours;* ***Size:*** *20 × 30 cm;*
Tools & Materials: *watercolor and pen*
on paper
The artist really likes drawing
in Middelburg, because it has
beautiful old facades. The
Oostchurch can be seen in the
distance.

Tips: "A few pedestrians and a
car provide a lively atmosphere."

10. Title: *Gent with the Belfort in*
Belgium; ***Place:*** *Gent, Belgium;*
Duration: *3 hours;* ***Size:*** *25 × 25 cm;*
Tools & Materials: *pen and watercolor*
From the year of 1000 till 1600
Gent was an important city in
Europe. The tower Belfort was
built in 1400.

Tips: "A few details on the
foreground make it clear this is a
building of the 16th century."

GENT januari 2014

Simon Holzman

French artist Simon Holzman lives in Paris, where he is currently working as an artist, graphic designer, and teacher. Through fine art, he seeks to uncover an indescribable and beautiful truth, a flesh and blood reality.

"

THROUGH FINE ART, I SEEK TO UNCOVER AN INDESCRIBABLE AND BEAUTIFUL TRUTH, A FLESH AND BLOOD REALITY.

"

Photography: Wei Shuai

 Simon Holzman's drawing tools and materials

I started painting with watercolor when I was 14. Now I tend to prefer oil painting for workshop works, but stick to watercolor for painting on the spot. You are your own tool, don't be the tool of the tool. A drop of ink, your finger, a piece of paper, nothing more is required for you to do something relevant, if you are a good artist. Buddhist monks paint with water on stones.

 Tools and materials recommended by Simon Holzman

- Conté pencil: they are soft and dark.
- Watercolor.
- Oil paint: brand Michael Harding, which seems to be more heavy in pigments, but turns out to be more economic.

👁 City in my eyes

I live in Paris hence I tend to draw what is in front of my eyes. I look forward to improving street scenes and making them real. I like to present personal views of my surroundings and sharing my feelings, making them easily and universally understood through a picture. Living in Paris, it has not proved difficult so far; it only requires time and the availability to get more information.

01

01. Title: *Avenue du Général Leclerc;*
Place: *Paris, France;* ***Duration:*** *1.5*
hours; ***Size:*** *38 × 25 cm;* ***Tools &***
Materials: *felt pen on a Moleskine*
notebook spread and brown ink
This is a view from a café.
The brown color was added
afterwards, which forms a strong
contrast to the original white
background, highlighting the main
body. What a bold color scheme!

Tips: "I have taken my time to
draw this one. I was seduced by
the details, maybe a little too
much!"

02   03

02. Title: *Rue des Plantes;* **Place:** *Paris, France;* **Duration:** *1.5 hours;* **Size:** *41 × 13 cm;* **Tools & Materials:** *watercolor and thin felt pen on a Moleskine notebook spread*
Sitting in a café in Paris, next to the window, the artist sketched both the inside and outside views of the place. He rendered the busy atmosphere by coloring the outside section, which makes a contrast with the quietness inside.

Tips: "A panoramic view on a Moleskine notebook. I like the format. It allows you to capture a broad vision. Watercolor added afterwards."

03. Title: *Bibliothèque François Mitterrand;* **Place:** *Paris, France;* **Duration:** *1.5 hours;* **Size:** *41 × 13 cm;* **Tools & Materials:** *watercolor and thin felt pen on a Moleskine notebook spread*
Done on the spot, the artist wanted to capture the feeling of the place, as it was under construction and obviously going to change day after day.

Tips: "Done on the spot. I did the line work very quickly, then added color washes above. "

0 2 FEV. 2009

28 JAN. 200...
Simon J. Holz

06

04. Title: *Place Denfert Rochereau;* **Place:** *Paris, France;* **Duration:** *1.5 hours;* **Size:** *38 × 25 cm;* **Tools & Materials:** *felt pen on a Moleskine notebook spread*
On a cold winter morning, the artist sat in a café and drew this work of art. He had a very good point of view and he's glad it turned out well.

Tips: "It was winter time. Snow was partially covering the sculpture of the place Denfert-Rochereau, Paris. I took a long time searching for the good lines. I wanted to make an accurate vision of the place."

05. Title: *Place Balard;* **Place:** *Paris, France;* **Duration:** *1.5 hours;* **Size:** *38 × 25 cm;* **Tools & Materials:** *felt pen on a Moleskine notebook spread*
From a café, looking south-east, the artist was focused on the perspective and peri-urban feeling, with the mix of steel, concrete, and vegetal elements.

Tips: "Just with a fine felt pen on a Moleskine notebook, I spent about two hours on the spot."

06. Title: *Rue des Grands Moulins;* **Place:** *Paris, France;* **Duration:** *1 - 2 hours;* **Size:** *38 × 25 cm;* **Tools & Materials:** *felt pen on a Moleskine notebook spread*
Construction zone: it has changed so much since. The artist still remembers the freezing moment, standing on that overpass. The view was great but, the temperature was low.

Tips: "With a felt pen on Moleskine notebook, I just jot down quickly the perspective and sank into the line work, right on the spot."

07. Title: *Le Vexin;* **Place:** *Jambville, France;* **Duration:** *1.5 hours;* **Size:** *41 × 13 cm;* **Tools & Materials:** *watercolor and thin felt pen on a Moleskine notebook spread*
This is the low view of a garden, simply drawn with paint on this Moleskine watercolor notebook.

Tips: "For this sketch I look forward to making things accurate."

08. Title: *La Chapelle-sous-Aubenas;* **Place:** *La Chapelle-sous-Aubenas, France;* **Duration:** *1.5 hours;* **Size:** *41 × 13 cm;* **Tools & Materials:** *watercolor and thin felt pen on a Moleskine notebook spread*
A summer day in a small town where the bright, dry colors were as interesting as the houses spread amongst the rocky landscape.

Tips: "I started using a permanent felt pen for the line work, then worked with watercolor right over, all done on the spot."

09. Title: *Pont Mirabeau;* **Place:** *Paris, France;* **Duration:** *1.5 hours;* **Size:** *38 × 25 cm;* **Tools & Materials:** *felt pen on a Moleskine notebook spread*
The artist sketched this on the spot on a hot, quiet summer day in Paris.

Tips: "I used a felt pen on a Moleskine notebook. The watercolor was added afterwards."

Yves Damin

Yves Damin was born in 1973, and was raised in a family of artists: his dad is also a painter. He spent his youth painting in France or abroad with his family, and then studied graphic design and illustration. He works as a graphic designer around Paris and keeps drawing as much as he can of what's around him.

Photography: Wei Shuai

EVEN IF YOU ARE IN A VERY FAMOUS PLACE, DRAW IT SINCERELY, WITH YOUR HEART AND YOUR EYES.

🧰 Yves Damin's drawing tools and materials

I usually carry with me a little pocket filled with a full range of fountain pens with various sizes, very soft pencils, small brushes and a tiny set of watercolors. I also have in my bag three sketchbooks (small, medium and large). With all of those tools, I can be ready to draw and paint anytime and anywhere!

✏ Tools and materials recommended by Yves Damin

• Staedler pigment ink liner: a full range of sizes is available, from ultra thin to wide, perfect for small details or large dark zones. The ink is indelible: so you can paint on it with watercolor and it won't fade.
• Leonard brushes: French manufacturer of professional brushes. They are really thin and are of high quality.
• Moleskine sketchbooks: excellent paper with resistance to water, several sizes, easy to carry everywhere and made with high quality.

👁 City in my eyes

I live in a lovely town in the west suburbs of Paris, Maisons Laffitte. It is a royal town, not far from Versailles. It means that the architecture is quite academic, with royal ornaments. Houses are built with white stones or red and oranges bricks. There are also many villas built with an Art-Deco style, mainly used for the doors and windows. Beautiful!

01. Title: *Piccadilly Circus, London;* **Place:** *London, UK;*
Duration: *2 hours;* **Size:** *29.7 × 21 cm;* **Tools & Materials:**
China ink and watercolor on paper

London is a really lively place, and the heart of
London is definitively Piccadilly Circus, where a lot
of buses and taxis move along. Regent Street is a very
elegant street with elegant buildings. The perspective
is a bit hard to draw because the street turns smoothly.
But that is a part of the challenge.

01

Yves Damin.

02. *Title:* Les Halles, Paris; *Place:* Paris, France; *Duration:* 2 hours; *Size:* 29.7 × 21 cm; *Tools & Materials:* China ink and watercolor on paper
The artist sketched this view from the top of the Pompidou Centre, one of the best French museums of modern art. There is an amazing view of Paris from up there, and people look so tiny.

Tips: "Start by building the perspective grid and focus on the main subject. Include people's shapes to give a scale."

03. *Title:* Hampstead Heath, London; *Place:* London, UK; *Duration:* 2 hours; *Size:* 29.7 × 21 cm; *Tools & Materials:* China ink and watercolor on paper
Hampstead is a little village in a huge town. The artist enjoys those tiny streets with beautiful shops and restaurants. Posh and glamourous, Hampstead is a great place to draw people doing their shopping.

Tips: "I did this sketch after shopping. I wanted to sit for a cup of tea. I started to draw, and it was cool. Sometimes you think about doing just a little sketch but at the end it turns out to be a proper scene."

04. *Title:* *Small Street of Hvar;* *Place:* *Hvar, Croatia;* *Duration:* *1.5 hours;* *Size:* *21 × 29.7 cm;* *Tools & Materials:* *China ink and watercolor on paper*

Hvar is a lovely village on the eponymous island of Hvar. Very well known by jet set people, and with a lot of famous clubs and bars, Hvar is also a beautiful village with tiny streets of stone houses, where visitors can easily get lost!

Tips: "One point perspective makes your drawing easier. It helps the eye to focus on what you want more easily."

05. *Title:* *The Roofs of Paris;* *Place:* *Paris, France;* *Duration:* *2 hours;* *Size:* *29.7 × 21 cm;* *Tools & Materials:* *China ink and watercolor on paper*

Paris is a big city with beautiful houses, but it is very interesting to climb on the roofs and see the city from above. Slate, zinc, bricks and cement are mixed in an amazing urban labyrinth.

Tips: "Don't get impressed by the quantity of details: start with global volumes that you will split in smaller volumes and so on."

04

05

06   Décembre 2013   Yves Damin

06. *Title:* *Villa Sully;* *Place:* *Maisons Laffitte, France;* *Duration:* *1.5 hours;* *Size:* *29.7 × 21 cm;* *Tools & Materials:* *China ink and watercolor on paper*
This house used to belong to a famous horse-race instructor. It is a massive villa with an Art Nouveau style, surrounded by green trees. It is a bit of excentric architecture: the house is massive, with several levels, and quite a few ornaments. It could have been a perfect place for Psycho or the Addams family, because of its mysterious atmosphere.

Tips: "Sometimes it's a good thing to have a dull weather. The same scene under a blue sky wouldn't have the same impact, gray sky enhances the atmosphere."

07. *Title:* *Horse Race at the Castle;* *Place:* *Maisons Laffitte, France;* *Duration:* *3 hours;* *Size:* *60 × 40 cm;* *Tools & Materials:* *China ink and watercolor on paper*
Maisons Laffitte is very well known for the castle and the horse races. That is why the artsit painted those two views, which represent the "elegance à la française."

Tips: "Try always to put a lively presence in your composition. Here, horses bring life and motion, which makes the scene less static."

08. *Title:* The Stables; *Place:* Maisons Laffitte, France; *Duration:* 1.5 hours; *Size:* 42 × 29.7 cm; *Tools & Materials:* China ink and watercolor on paper

There are quite a few stables around the artist's house, and this one is very nice: there is a big courtyard, nice wooden houses and beautiful trees. It's a peaceful place where horses live happily.

Tips: "Sometimes you can go with a friend. That's what happened here: It was freezing, but being with another sketcher was a good motivation for standing for an hour in the cold wind!"

09. *Title:* Southwark Bridge, London; *Place:* London, UK; *Duration:* 1.5 hours; *Size:* 29.7 × 21 cm; *Tools & Materials:* China ink and watercolor on paper

The artist sketched this view from… the beach, in Central London! It was freezing because it was Christmas, but he really wanted to bring back this skyline in his sketchbook.

Tips: "Take your time to find the best point of view. Here, I was looking for a particuliar angle, so I walked by the Thames and found the stairs."

Ecuries Albric
Maisons Laffitte, novembre 2013

Southwark Bridge

Yves Da…

Yves Damin
13 février 2011

Yves Damin.

Yves Damin.

11

10. *Title:* Cruise on the Adriatic; *Place:* Hvar, Croatia; *Duration:* 1.5 hours; *Size:* 21 × 29.7 cm; *Tools & Materials:* China ink and watercolor on paper

During summer holidays, the artist and his wife traveled in the Croatian islands. They sailed on big boats under the sun. This work is a lively souvenir from those beautiful trips on cargos.

Tips: "Even if you only have a little time, don't be shy to get your sketchbook. Don't wait for the perfect landscape to draw, but see life as a playground to practice. Trips are a great experience."

11. *Title:* Nice Villa; *Place:* Maisons Laffitte, France; *Duration:* 1 hour; *Size:* 29.7 × 21 cm; *Tools & Materials:* China ink and watercolor on paper

Around the artist's house, there are fantastic villas. This one is one of them, a kind of Alpine house with typical shape of roof and windows, which is quite unusual around Paris.

Tips: "Explore around your place. Don't wait for the next holiday. Just go around the corner to find local places to draw."

Fabio Barilari

Fabio Barilari is an architect, illustrator and painter. As an architect (degree with honors in Architecture Design at the Sapienza University of Rome) he has collaborated as a freelancer with several prestigious studios, specializing in complex architectural and urban structures. In 1996 he founded "FABIO BARILARI ARCHITETTI." Since 2008, Fabio Barilari has developed his professional activity, extending his research beyond architecture to sectors related to illustration, graphics and painting. Fabio's personal work has been widely published in national and international architectural books, magazines and websites.

> " SOMETIMES, THE PLACE IS VERY EASY TO EXPRESS IN ALL ITS BEAUTY. "

📥 Fabio Barilari's drawing tools and materials

I have always used a great variety of tools and materials, as I've always been very interested in experimenting. However, I particularly like to use the following:
Pen: Koh-I-Noor Fiber Professional series: n° 0.2 and 0.3 in particular/Uniball eye micro.
Pencil: Rotring 600G 0.5/Faber-Castel Propelling Pencing 1.8/Lamy scribble 3.15.
Paper: Moleskine watercolor and Fabriano Acquarello Grana fina – cold-pressed.

✏ Tools and materials recommended by Fabio Barilari

- Watercolors: Winsor & Newton Professional. I have 3 different boxes: A W&N metal box, 16 colors half Godet, to bring in the pocket; A W&N wood box, 26 half Godet, to work on the table and a special W&N wood 5 big Godet on ceramic, for the biggest and most important works.
- Oil Pastels: Sennelier. They have a fantastic selection of colors, made of great pigments. I particularly appreciate the way you can melt and mix them on paper, using fingers.
- Brushes: Winsor & Newton – Finest Sable/Da Vinci. In both cases, I experienced excellent results both in bringing the color on paper or canvas and ergonomic handle.
- Markers: Faber-Castell Pitt big brush. They have a very good list of colors and quality of material. They are also

very ergonomic when being handled.
- Acrylic: Golden Open/Liquitex, possibly with some additives to slow the drying process and to increase the brightness of color.

👁 City in my eyes

I am an architect, which means that I establish a special relationship with the city I draw. I live in Rome, but I have the same approach in every place I visit. It's not just about the architecture; I'm also particularly interested in daily life within places. So I can draw both architectural masterpieces and minor details with the same interest, if I feel that they can say something special about the place I am working on.

Photography: Fabio Barilari

01

02

01-02. *Title: Roma – Santa Maria della Pace; Place: Rome, Italy; Duration: 4 hours; Size: 45.5 × 30.5 cm (above); Tools & Materials: pen and watercolor on paper*

This is a quite little and hidden church in Rome, but one of the most important ones. The facade and the little square in front of it were built in the Baroque Period by Pietro da Cortona, one of the leading architects of that age, together with Bernini and Borromini. In all the Baroque architecture, light and shadows create beautiful drawings of the building's rich geometries.

Tips: "Rome is also a city of strong sunlight and deep shadows. The Baroque architecture expresses this characteristic more than architecture of all the other architectural periods."

03. *Title:* *Essaouira;* *Place:* *Essaouira,*
Morocco; *Duration:* *1 day;* *Size:*
45.5 × 30.5 cm; *Tools & Materials:* *ink*
brush and watercolor on paper
This is a view of the Atlantic
Ocean, from the "Promenade,"
the walk over the walls facing the
sea in this ancient little town in the
south of Morocco.

Tips: "In this case, I was deeply
impressed by the strong mood
of this little town in Morocco.
Instead of the architecture,
the details, and the sea view,
I was more interested in
expressing this silent and
hidden atmosphere through the
drawing."

04. *Title:* *Roma – Campo dè Fiori;*
Place: *Rome, Italy;* *Duration:* *2 days;*
Size: *45.5 × 30.5 cm;* *Tools & Materials:*
pen and watercolor on paper
Campo dè Fiori is one of the most
famous piazzas in Rome and the
statue represents Giordano Bruno,
a monk and philosopher declared
heretic by the Vatican and burned
at the stake in 1600. His bronze
statue, erected in 1889, looks with
harshness exactly in the direction
of the Vatican Dome.

Tips: "I draw everything I see in
the scene. It's only later, using the
color, that I put the main focus
on something special: an object,
a color or simply a corner of the
street."

05. *Title: San Francisco – Street;* ***Place:*** *San Francisco, USA;* ***Duration:*** *2 days;* ***Size:*** *45.5 × 30.5 cm;* ***Tools & Materials:*** *pen and watercolor on paper*

There's a beautiful mix of colors of the buildings, intricate grids of the cables above the streets, and a quiet and peaceful atmosphere all around. Using the gray ink, the artist can both create strong shadows and put the focus on some details of the image. It's a good way to tell something more about the place.

Tips: "This drawing shows clearly my personal idea of context drawing: the electrical lines cut the skies of San Francisco in beautiful and complex geometries."

06. *Title: Roma – Area del Teatro Marcello;* ***Place:*** *Rome, Italy;* ***Duration:*** *1.5 days;* ***Size:*** *45.5 × 30.5 cm;* ***Tools & Materials:*** *pen and watercolor on paper*

The aritst made this work standing on the ancient Rome layer: this means, around six meters below the contemporary city. People may experience this strange point of view in several areas in the centre of Rome. This is the area just in front of the Teatro Marcello, near the Campidoglio hill.

Tips: "I made this drawing six meters below ground level and looking up. That's the level of ancient Rome."

06

Time Off

a blue whale song

MONTEREY

Time Off

PIER

TIME ~~ALWAYS~~ SMILES IN MY HAND

07

somewhere out there

Time Off

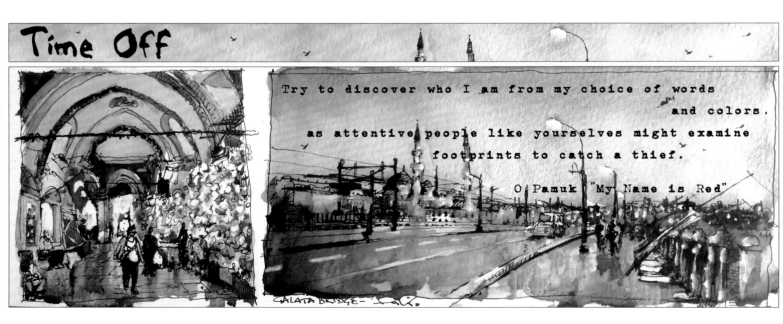

Try to discover who I am from my choice of words
and colors,
as attentive people like yourselves might examine
footprints to catch a thief.

O. Pamuk "My Name is Red"

GALATA BRIDGE -

09

77

Time Off

I dreamed of you last night   and saw

              I heard your laugh   bet

11

r beautiful face

all those noisy shadows

07-10. *Title:* Time Off Series; *Place:* San Francisco, USA; Monterey, USA; Istanbul, Turkey; *Duration:* 2 days; *Size:* 42 × 13 cm; *Tools & Materials:* pen and watercolor on paper

This is a series of works based on short and immediate texts. In this project, the relation between the drawing and the written language aims at describing and marking the readers' feeling, the deep emotion and mood of the narrated places with immediate images. This series is currently on-going.

Tips: "'Time Off' is a long-term project in which I am interested in connecting drawings and words with no other meanings than their affinity in mood and sound."

11. *Title:* Ponza; *Place:* Ponza, Italy; *Duration:* 2 hour; *Size:* 42 × 13 cm; *Tools & Materials:* pen and watercolor on paper

This is a view of the beautiful and colorful old harbor of Ponza, one of the islands in front of the coasts in the south region of Rome.

Tips: "Sometimes, the place is very easy to express in all its beauty. This is the case for Ponza island's little harbor."

Guy Moll

Guy Moll is a French retired teacher whose hobbies are photography and painting. Five years ago he joined the "Urban Sketchers" group and began to send his works to the group on Flickr. He participated in the International Urban Sketching Symposium in Lisbon in 2011, and in the French National Sketch Crawl in Lyon in 2013. He paints mostly in Portugal, France, and Spain, and usually creates his sketches in one or two hours using different media. For more information, please visit his website: www.guymoll.com. sapo.pt.

🧰 Guy Moll's drawing tools and materials

For my on-location urban sketches, I currently use ballpoint, pencil or pen, watercolor, sketching books and a good pliant chair. The ballpoint is more difficult than the pencil because it must be used with a light hand: it is virtually impossible to go back with no scrub. The same problem happens with the pigment liner, the most difficult of all drawing tools. The pencil must be 2 or 3 B, not too hard.

🖌 Tools and materials recommended by Guy Moll

• A ballpoint such as the BIC black or sepia. It's easy to find everywhere for rapid implementation and indelible for watercolor.
• A pencil, or a pen (Artpen by Rotring – but this brand doesn't provide indelible Indian ink...) or a pigment liner (Staedler 0.1 to 0.5 or Pigma micron 0.05 to 0.5).
• Watercolor (such as Sennelier, Windsor & Newton or Schminke...) with brushes (Petit Gris from Isabey) and brushes including watercan (Pentel). These last ones are very useful because there is no need to transport water.
• Sketching books: different brands like Canson artbook or Arches. Actually, for panoramic sketches I use a Derwent watercolor book (43 × 18 cm). I like also very much a Moleskine watercolor book (21 × 13 cm) that makes 42 × 13 cm open with the best paper for watercoloring. The quality of the paper is very important: the size of my sketches is not so big and a grammage of 150 to 200 is enough.

👁 City in my eyes

Faro is evidently my favorite place to draw. I draw quite every day in the city: old houses, beautiful doors and places and a lot of tourists all the year. Faro has no winter and it is easy to sit everywhere with my pliant chair.

Photography: Guy Moll

LISBOA - PORTUGAL

Guy Moll 04.13

THEATRE CHARLES DULLIN

GLACI

Guy Moll

> URBAN SKETCHING CAN
> ALSO SHOW THE DIFFERENT
> MOMENTS OF CITY LIFE.

01. Title: *Lisbon – Portugal 1;* **Place:** *Lisbon, Portugal;* **Duration:** *1.5 hours;* **Size:** *30 × 15 cm;* **Tools & Materials:** *BIC and watercolor on Derwent 165 g paper block*

It's taken from the Rossio Square, the main place of the centre of the city. On the left is the D. Maria Theater. The artist attempted to show the busy atmosphere of the place.

Tips: "This is a very busy place and, I put a lot of people which I chose one by one... They give some depth and life to the sketch."

02. Title: *Chambéry – France;* **Place:** *Chambéry, France;* **Duration:** *1.5 hours;* **Size:** *42 × 13 cm;* **Tools & Materials:** *BIC and watercolor on Moleskine watercolor block*

This is an on-location BIC and watercolor sketch, on a Moleskine watercolor panoramic sketchbook. Both open pages measure 42 cm long. Like in his other sketches, the artist drew a lot of people, done one by one.

Tips: "Using shadows and sunlight, I lead the eye to the main building, the municipal theater, on the left side of the sketch."

03. *Title:* Carvoeiro – Portugal; *Place:* Carvoeiro, Portugal; *Duration:* 1.5 hours; *Size:* 42 × 13 cm; *Tools & Materials:* BIC and watercolor on Moleskine watercolor block

This is an idyllic place. A lot of couples in bathing suits contributed to this unusual sketch. Sketchers often tend to end the panoramic sketches on the right side, here with the biggest houses.

Tips: "Water always gives a good complement to the sketches, attracting people and giving life to the old stones of the cities."

04. *Title: Olhão – Portugal; Place: Olhão, Portugal; Duration: 1.5 hours; Size: 42 × 13 cm; Tools & Materials: BIC and watercolor on Moleskine watercolor block*

The market (selling fish, fruit and vegetables) is one of the busiest parts of Olhão, principally on Saturdays with a lot of buyers and tourists. The scene is very nice to sketch.

Tips: "Café terraces are delightful to sketch; people are sitting, moving less and are easy to catch."

05

06

07

05. *Title:* Lectoure – France; *Place:* Lectoure, France; *Duration:* 1.5 hours; *Size:* 21 × 13 cm; *Tools & Materials:* BIC and watercolor on Moleskine watercolor block

This work was made on one page only. Lectoure is a beautiful town in southwest of France: the sun, gastronomy and old villages. The Roman cathedral adds interest to this sketch.

Tips: "If there are trees, I always include them, giving more life to the sketch."

06. *Title:* Ferragudo – Portugal; *Place:* Ferragudo, Portugal; *Duration:* 1.5 hours; *Size:* 42 × 13 cm; *Tools & Materials:* BIC and watercolor on Moleskine watercolor block

In this panoramic sketch the artist tried to put the depth as best as possible, with the biggest city of Portimão in the far. The scene is really nice to enjoy!

Tips: "Lakes or seas give the opportunity of reflections in the water, always very nice in a sketch."

07. *Title:* Faro – Portugal 2; *Place:* Faro, Portugal; *Duration:* 1.5 hours; *Size:* 42 × 13 cm; *Tools & Materials:* BIC and watercolor on Moleskine watercolor block

Near the marina, with beautiful palm trees, painted two years ago. Now the trees have died, like most of them in the mediterranean countries, eaten by insects coming from Egypt... A pity for photographers and sketchers...

Tips: "The use of panoramic view is essential (the human eye sees 180°) and the Moleskine aquarelle block is the best I know for this purpose."

08. *Title:* Kaysersberg – France; *Place:* Kaysersberg, France; *Duration:* 1.5 hours; *Size:* 30 × 17 cm; *Tools & Materials:* BIC and watercolor on Derwent 165 g paper block

The old town of Kaysersberg is built at the foot of the ruined middle-age castle. It attracts a lot of tourists visiting from spring to autumn each year.

Tips: "The clouds are made with a lot of water and a little color (yellow and crimson)."

08

LISBONNE - CAMÖENS - NOËL

FARO

09. *Title: Lisbon – Portugal 2; **Place:** Lisbon, Portugal; **Duration:** 1.5 hours; **Size:** 42 × 13 cm; **Tools & Materials:** BIC and watercolor on Moleskine watercolor block*

This was created in December, on the Carmo place, which is one of the busiest places of Lisbon. The pine tree is rare to see here because it appears only at Christmas time.

Tips: "Urban sketching can also show the different moments of city life. Here, Christmas is suggested by the pine tree."

10. *Title: Faro – Portugal 1; **Place:** Faro, Portugal; **Duration:** 1.5 hours; **Size:** 42 × 13 cm; **Tools & Materials:** BIC and watercolor on Moleskine watercolor block*

This is one of the most interesting places of Faro, with its cafés and people always passing by. The artist did not want to include the red lorry but it did not move during more than half an hour. Finally he let it stay there.

Tips: "This red color of the truck was a good idea, giving more interest to the sketch."

11. *Title: Silves – Portugal 1; **Place:** Silves, Portugal; **Duration:** 1.5 hours; **Size:** 30 × 15 cm; **Tools & Materials:** BIC and watercolor on Derwent 165 g paper block*

The architecture and landscapes in this old Moorish village are so charming that the artist decided to sketch it from different angles, and this was one of them. Really nice!

Tips: "I like to choose a couple or some other people that I put in the forefront to help achieve depth of the sketch."

11

SILVES

12. *Title:* Eguisheim - France; *Place:* Eguisheim, France; *Duration:* 1.5 hours; *Size:* 30 × 17 cm; *Tools & Materials:* BIC and watercolor on Derwent 165 g paper block

Typical houses and a splendid fountain inspired the artist a lot. This little village has been chosen as "the Preferred Village of France" by the French people on television in 2013.

Tips: "The sun and shadows give more contrast to the sketch."

13. *Title:* Faro – Portugal 3; *Place:* Faro, Portugal; *Duration:* 1.5 hours; *Size:* 42 × 13 cm; *Tools & Materials:* BIC and watercolor on Moleskine watercolor block

This panoramic sketch depicts a nice place with one of the numerous newspapers kiosks of the city. The scene is full of details of city life that add vitality to the sketch.

Tips: "I try not to forget all the little details of the city life: cars, kiosks, street lamps, mailboxes, trashes…"

14. *Title:* Lisbon – Portugal 3; *Place:* Lisbon, Portugal; *Duration:* 1.5 hours; *Size:* 30 × 21 cm; *Tools & Materials:* BIC and watercolor on normal 100 g paper

This sketch was made during the International Urban Sketching Symposium in Lisbon in 2011. The place is the same as the sketch "Lisbon-Portugal 2" (taken from the opposite side).

Tips: "The sketch itself is done with a few pencil strokes. I let the brush give all the movements."

15. *Title:* Colmar – France 1; *Place:* Colmar, France; *Duration:* 1.5 hours; *Size:* 29 × 21 cm; *Tools & Materials:* BIC and watercolor on watercolor 200 g paper

In the centre of the city, there are a lot of beautiful houses like this, the Maison Pfister (built in the 16th century), with its "oriels." It deserves to be recorded by sketchers.

Tips: "I like tourist groups. They always give a lot of movement and are not difficult to catch: they stay for sufficient time on the spot when they watch the descriptions on the guide."

14

15

Natalija Nikolceva

Natalija Nikolceva lives and works in Riga, Latvia. She started painting from early childhood, but it turned into a real passion in 2000, when she met her art tutor, who is now still her tutor and a true friend. Natalija has a Master's Degree in IT and software development is her main job. Since the job allows her to work flexibly, sometimes she travels around with her laptop and watercolor set.

TRY TO SEE YOUR HOMETOWN OR CITY YOU LIVE IN THROUGH DIFFERENT EYES, AS IF YOU WERE A TOURIST IN IT.

🧰 Natalija Nikolceva's drawing tools and materials

Since I work with different painting and drawing techniques, and not only in urban sketch, I use a wide range of materials and tools like watercolors, ink, oil, pastels, fineliners, as well as different surfaces like paper (simple, watercolor, pastel paper), cardboard, canvas, etc. In my opinion, even if an artist prefers one drawing or painting technique, it is very useful and even very important to make experiments with different techniques as it enriches his or her favorite technique when he or she returns to it.

✏ Tools and materials recommended by Natalija Nikolceva

- Watercolors: White Nights – it is my favorite brand made in St. Petersburg, Russia. However, I also use some other brands like Van Gogh from Holland, as well as some Italian brands. White Nights are made from natural pigments so the colors look very natural.
- Fineliner set with different line widths: Rotring or Faber-Castell, used for contour drawing, clear and vibrant, cheaper and convenient.
- Brushes: Chinese calligraphic brushes have thin elastic tips and are very soft. Brush strokes are always unpredictable, unique and very picturesque, and it is possible to make wide as well as thin strokes. I also use some European brushes like Lukas, Da Vinci, etc.
- Watercolor paper: Any good quality watercolor paper. For urban sketching, I prefer European paper with smooth texture (such as French Canson, some British and German brands), and it's better for fineliners.
- Photo camera: Sony Rx-100. It could be any small camera that fits into a bag, used to capture some details of landscape or architecture to complete the sketches later.

👁 City in my eyes

Venice is the city of infinite inspiration. I could keep drawing it over and over again. Although it is not my favorite city because of tourist crowds, its architecture, channels, art everywhere around, cafés and delicious coffee are all attractive to me.

Photography: Natalija Nikolceva

01. *Title: Rundale; Place: Rundale, Latvia; Duration: 40 minutes; Size: 25 × 37 cm; Tools & Materials: watercolor, fineliner and watercolor paper*

This is an amazing palace in the middle of nowhere. It was built by a famous Italian architect ordered by Russian Empress Anna Ioannovna for her favorite Duke of Courland Biron. It's a wonderful place for painting in the centre of Latvia near the little villages.

Tips: "When sketching I start with a large, soft, wet brush. I make a very light and free sketch to designate color spots, light and shadows. Then I wait some time until the paper is mostly dry, but not completely."

02. *Title:* *Basilica di San Marco;* ***Place:*** *Venice, Italy;* ***Duration:*** *30 minutes;* ***Size:*** *13 × 21 cm;* ***Tools & Materials:*** *watercolor, fineliner and watercolor paper*

This is a main symbol and a centre of Venice. The architecture there is very complicated and interesting for drawing. Every detail can become a completed composition. The cathedral is full of statues of saints and decorative elements.

Tips: "For a second layer I use fineliners (ink pen or technical pen) and draw contours. And when the contour is dry, I fluently make a third layer using a thin brush to complete the work – set more precise shadows, bright spots and accents."

03. *Title:* *Horse in the Centre of Venice;* ***Place:*** *Venice, Italy;* ***Duration:*** *30 minutes;* ***Size:*** *16 × 23 cm;* ***Tools & Materials:*** *watercolor, fineliner and watercolor paper*

Venice – a city filled with water, boats, pigeons, fine arts, architecture, etc. It is not the artist's favorite city because of the number of tourists, but there is always something to paint. This has been created to display the mood and the city atmosphere.

Tips: "The most important thing is to feel free and not be afraid of spoiling anything, as inaccuracies can always be fixed and sometimes those inaccuracies can even give charm to your work."

02

03

04. *Title:* Miera Street, Riga; *Place:* Riga, Latvia; *Duration:* 1 hour; *Size:* 38 × 29 cm; *Tools & Materials:* Indian ink and watercolor paper

It was an interesting experiment working with Indian ink. In this work the artist used the twigs of trees instead of brushes. The drawing was made on location. This is one of the painter's favorite lovely old houses in her hometown Riga. The house already looks haunted, but there are still people living there.

Tips: "Try as many materials as possible and improvise! Something like tree branches as brush, or even coffee in a café as watercolor. I heard about one artist who painted using vegetables. Beetroot, for example, is perfect."

05. *Title:* London Street; *Place:* London, UK; *Duration:* 30 minutes; *Size:* 23 × 20 cm; *Tools & Materials:* watercolor, fineliner and watercolor paper

This is one of the neat streets of London. The artist lived in London for about four months. London is a city that obviously has its own characters, mood, and atmosphere. This city looks like the old tidy lady in a white cap.

Tips: "Traveling a lot will bring you fresh impressions and help you gain experience. Just have a compact watercolor set, sketchbook and a brush in your bag, or any materials you prefer."

06

07

06. Title: *Bangkok;* **Place:** *Bangkok, Thailand;* **Duration:** *30 minutes;* **Size:** *13 × 18 cm;* **Tools & Materials:** *watercolor, fineliner and watercolor paper*

The artist lived in Thailand for two months. It was a wonderful experience and a chance to look at a different culture from the inside. This is a beautiful country with beautiful and smiling people. Drawing this country is a real pleasure. The artist loves more quiet, small places more than bustling megapolises, but in the big cities there is always something to paint.

Tips: "Sometimes to live in another country for a while is very useful to see the country from within, as if you were a citizen with everyday worries. It allows you to discover interesting things."

07. Title: *Houses in Venice;* **Place:** *Venice, Italy;* **Duration:** *30 minutes;* **Size:** *18 × 13 cm;* **Tools & Materials:** *watercolor, fineliner and watercolor paper*

The most enjoyable part of painting and drawing what surrounds us are the details in people's faces, lingerie in a back yard, details of buildings such as roofs, windows, statues, decorations, etc. These things are what the memories of different places consist of.

Tips: "All motions are very quick and free. I try to focus more on the mood of a landscape than on reality."

08. Title: *Riga's Roof in Black and White;* **Place:** *Riga, Latvia;* **Duration:** *15 minutes;* **Size:** *15 × 20 cm;* **Tools & Materials:** *fineliner and paper*

There is one little tower on the roof. Interesting! Riga is a very old city. Almost all houses in the center of Riga have their own special details: little towers on the roofs, the clock on these towers, houses for birds, and a special wind vane; the most important thing is their own history.

Tips: "Try to see your hometown or city you live in through different eyes, as if you were a tourist in it. It allows you to discover many new things in your city."

08

09. *Title: One of the Millions of Channels in Venice; **Place:** Venice, Italy; **Duration:** 30 minutes; **Size:** 13 × 23 cm; **Tools & Materials:** watercolor, fineliner and watercolor paper*

It was one of the few rare quiet corners of Venice, and it was a drawing for real pleasure. The water channels of Venice create a special atmosphere in the city. On both sides along the channels are beautiful palaces; each palace is particular in its own way.

Tips: "Try to pay attention to the light, shadows and reflection, if you draw water. Everything should be reflected – objects, light, and color."

Arno Hartmann

Arno Hartmann is a graduate in Architecture from the Faculty of Architecture and Urban Planning of the University of Siegen (Germany). He was an independent architect with "LHVH Architekten" before he started as a freelance graphic artist and web designer. Since 2009, he has been an instructor of perspective drawing at the "Summer Academy Harz." Since 2013, Arno has been an assistant professor for architectural presentation at TU Dortmund University. His drawings and watercolors focus on historical architecture in cities in and around central Europe, and he is a member of Urban Sketchers Germany.

OFTEN DRAMATIC ANGLES MAKE A PICTURE MORE INTERESTING.

🧰 Arno Hartmann's drawing tools and materials

I generally use Faber Castell Pitt pen, Faber Castell 9000 HB pencil and two kinds of sketching books. A very helpful tool is my fishing chair. It is a folding stool attached to a backpack, so once you've sat down, you have your belongings at hand and you don't have to worry about pick pockets.

✏️ Tools and materials recommended by Arno Hartmann

- Pen: I use a Faber Castell Pitt artist pen, normally with an S tip. Sometimes I use the F or the B tip, which has a brush-like feeling to it.
- Pencil: With softer pencils, my drawings tend to smear, so my preferred pencil is a Faber Castell 9000 HB. It's very stable, even when I press hard to get dark strokes.
- Sketching book: The Boesner 170 gsm sketchbook, 27 × 35 cm, has a nice linen cover and the paper has a beautiful, slightly rough surface. However, one has to deal with a slight yellow tinge. Stillman & Birn's "Alpha Series" sketchbook has the same size. Their paper is finer and whiter, but the fake leather cover sticks if your hands are sweaty in hot weather.
- Eraser: My eraser is a white Faber-Castell 7081N vinyl eraser. It doesn't leave any traces on the paper and it's quite soft, so that the paper doesn't get too scratched.
- Pencil sharpener: Most urban sketchers use a simple pocket knife to sharpen their pencils. But I always have my Dahle 155 pencil sharpener with its crank and

chipping drawer from my old days as an architect. Thus, the pencil tip stays nice and round.
- Watercolor box: Lukas watercolor box with 24 cups. Don't keep it too clean – always mix your colors.

👁 City in my eyes

My home region is Franconia in Northern Bavaria. Many small towns there have kept their medieval appearance with their half-timbered townhouses. Some bigger ones are baroque jewels, like Würzburg or Bamberg, both of which have World Heritage status. Embedded in a landscape characterized by low mountain ranges, river valleys, and hardwood forests, it's also one of Germany's most prominent beer and wine-producing regions.

Photography: Arno Hartmann

01. *Title:* Würzburg Residence; *Place:* Würzburg, Germany; *Duration:* 1.25 hours; *Size:* 35 × 27 cm; *Tools & Materials:* Faber Castell HB pencil and Lukas watercolor on Boesner 170 gsm sketchbook and sky color added digitally

In contrast to the territory over which the prince-bishops ruled 250 years ago, their Würzburg Residence is a really large castle. Napoleon called it "the nicest parsonage in Europe." The blazing afternoon sun on the west facade made some facets of the mansard roofs shine brightly.

Tips: "Sketching only a part of a building can result in a good drawing, too. Symmetrical buildings are especially much more interesting if you choose an asymmetrical image section. And no one will compare the left side of your drawing with the right side…"

02

02. *Title:* St. Vitus Cathedral; *Place:* Prague, Czech; *Duration:* 1.75 hours; *Size:* 27 × 35 cm; *Tools & Materials:* Faber Castell HB pencil and Lukas watercolor on Boesner 170 gsm sketchbook

On the Hradčany, the southern elevation of St. Vitus Cathedral and its east end are good choices to draw. Gothic churches are always difficult to draw, because under all the vertical lines and buttresses the artist must keep the rhythm and the symmetry of the main structure in mind. Note the main tower: It's like the builders decided to switch to the Renaissance style from one day to the other.

> **Tips:** "Try to plan your visit to a certain site: When will the sun shine on the facade you want to draw? Will there be a shadowy place to sit?"

03

04

03. *Title:* Möllenbeck Monastery; *Place:* Rinteln, Germany; *Duration:* 2 hours; *Size:* 54 × 35 cm; *Tools & Materials:* Faber Castell HB pencil and Lukas watercolor on Boesner 170 gsm sketchbook

Möllenbeck Monastery today is a youth hostel and a very good starting point for trips to the Weser Uplands and the buildings of the Weser Renaissance. The southwest corner gives a good impression of the whole complex. As seen in the upper left corner, the artist often does a fast concept sketch of the situation to make sure the composition will fit the paper.

> **Tips:** "For double page drawings, look for contiguous pages in your thread-bound sketchbook. The break will be much less visible. You can skip some pages and fill them later."

04. *Title:* Kurtheater Bad Kissingen; *Place:* Bad Kissingen, Germany; *Duration:* 1 hour; *Size:* 35 × 27 cm; *Tools & Materials:* Faber Castell HB pencil and Lukas watercolor on Boesner 170 gsm sketchbook

The small Bavarian spa town Bad Kissingen has its own little opera house, the "Kurtheater," built in 1904, with a beautiful art nouveau interior. The building's complex shapes are quite difficult to draw and shade.

> **Tips:** "Don't erase flagpoles, signs or lampposts from your sketch. Try to embed them into your composition."

05. Title: *National Theatre;* ***Place:***
Prague, Czech; ***Duration:*** *1.5 hours;*
Size: *35 × 27 cm;* ***Tools & Materials:***
Faber Castell HB pencil and Lukas
watercolor on Boesner 170 gsm
sketchbook

The National Theatre (Národní
divadlo), completed in 1881
in Renaissance Revival style, is
one of the many highlights on
the Vltava River in Prague. The
dramatic perspective from the
nearby Most Legií Bridge and the
mighty roof add to the impressive
appearance of the building. It
was a challenge to depict the rich
facade without getting lost in the
details.

Tips: "It's not necessary to draw
everything you see. Often the
non finito has its special charm,
too."

06. *Title:* Bamberg Town Hall; *Place:* Bamberg, Germany; *Duration:* 1.5 hours; *Size:* 35 × 27 cm; *Tools & Materials:* Faber Castell HB pencil and Lukas watercolor on Boesner 170 gsm sketchbook

Bamberg's old town is a World Heritage site. The old city hall was built on an island in the middle of the Regnitz River, exactly on the border between the prince-bishop's territory and the citizens' quarters. When drawing renaissance and baroque spires, there is always the danger of getting lost in the details and depicting them bigger than they really are.

Tips: "Try to force yourself to sketch faster. It helps you concentrate on the most important parts and prevents you from getting lost in the details of your drawing object."

07. *Title:* Burg Runkel; *Place:* Runkel, Germany; *Duration:* 2 hours; *Size:* 35 × 27 cm; *Tools & Materials:* Faber Castell HB pencil and Lukas watercolor on Stillman & Birn "Alpha Series" sketchbook

Runkel is one of the many beautiful towns and castles along the Lahn river in central Germany. Sitting on a piece of land near a barrier weir, the artist and three more urban sketchers drew the panorama with the two castles, the old town, the bridge and the river. The hatchings and the watercolor of the sky are more an interpretation of the intense view than an accurate depiction of the surfaces and the weather.

Tips: "It often pays off to walk around a place for a while before you start drawing. Thus you'll find viewing angles you would have missed otherwise."

08. *Title:* Klütz, Bothmer Castle; *Place:* Klütz, Germany; *Duration:* 2.5 hours; *Size:* 35 × 27 cm; *Tools & Materials:* Faber Castell HB pencil and Lukas watercolor on Stillman & Birn "Alpha Series" sketchbook

Bothmer Castle, one of Northern Germany's biggest castle complexes, was built in 1732 for the British king's advisor. The artist went there in the hope that the long-term restoration work was finally completed. It was not. So he did a series of partial views, and made the construction site a part of his drawings.

Tips: "The best way to deal with a large ensemble is to start with a series of many smaller drawings from many angles."

09. *Title:* Rinteln Münchhausenhof; *Place:* Rinteln, Germany; *Duration:* 1 hour; *Size:* 27 × 20 cm; *Tools & Materials:* Faber Castell HB pencil and Lukas watercolor on Stillman & Birn "Alpha Series" sketchbook

The building in the foreground is said to be the smallest building of the Weser Renaissance. The whole court is named after the noble family Münchhausen, with their most prominent member, the "Lying Baron," an inventor of a series of tall tales.

Tips: "Often dramatic angles make a picture more interesting."

Moo Hyun Chung

Moo was born and raised in the Dominican Republic and is of South Korean descent. He draws as much as he breathes. The artist graduated from Altos de Chavón School of Design with a degree in Fine Arts/Illustration and has an MA in Experience Design from SADI. Sketching on location is one of his biggest passions, others of which are illustration and humor. He blends these manias and produces content for several of his participating blogs such as Daily Critter and Unhappy People.

> *REGARDLESS OF WHAT TOOLS YOU HAVE, OBSERVATION IS PARAMOUNT!*

🧰 Moo Hyun Chung's drawing tools and materials

I will let the composition decide where I will sit and what medium to use. For example, when I sketched the Eiffel Tower from below, the only shade provided was from the tower. But as time passed, the shadow moved, forcing me to change where I was sitting. It was still a very fun experience and the result was much more satisfying.

✒ Tools and materials recommended by Moo Hyun Chung

- Observation: This is the number one tool I recommend. Merging yourself with the environment is essential for a more successful reflection on your sketchbook. Don't just see and copy, observe and feel.
- Ink: This is the most common tool. No specific brands, it's not about the brand but about what you can make with it. And by ink, I also mean a fountain pen and/or a dip pen.
- Watercolor: The watercolor kit I use is the Koi brand from Sakura. It brings quite a wide variety of colors and it even includes a water brush, which is very useful when you don't want to carry many things.
- Brushes and water brushes: These are essentials to work around with ink and the watercolors. It is also a great way to get different stroke values and create a more dynamic narration of the view.
- Fountain pen and dip pens: Last but not the least, these are what I am most comfortable with. Please note that I do not mention pencils, because I prefer to jump into the sketch and have zero second thoughts.

👁 City in my eyes

The city I have drawn the most is my hometown, Santo Domingo. Santo Domingo is great; you can enjoy the turquoise hues of the beach while relaxing with an ice-cold beer and sketching or you can go to the colonial ruins inside the city and be marveled by the feeling of traveling to the past. Parts of the city are covered with only trees and hills; take a deep breath of fresh air and start sketching here. The city itself is inhabited by a wide variety of people, for Santo Domingo welcomes everyone from all around the world.

Photography: Moo Hyun Chung

01. Title: *Louvre Lover;* **Place:** *Paris, France;* **Duration:** *1.5 hours;* **Size:** *11 × 9 cm;* **Tools & Materials:** *watercolor, pencil and ink on paper*
One of the biggest challenges imposed in this stage was the swarm of tourists that walk about every single second of the day. But indeed, this challenge is what makes outlining the Louvre so delicious.

Tips: "I started by creating big blocks of shapes using watercolor to structure the composition before starting. After it completely dried, I used ink to draw on top of the shapes."

03

02. *Title: Eiffel in Love; **Place:** Paris, France; **Duration:** 1.75 hours; **Size:** 9 × 11 cm; **Tools & Materials:** watercolor and ink on paper*
Some of the places you might sketch are commonly photographed and drawn. The artist had this in mind when he went to the Eiffel Tower, and had already decided that he would try to get a different point of view. He wanted to make it a more personal experience by looking for an uncommon angle.

Tips: "For those repeated themes I'd like to try a different view angle to give the drawing more personal features."

03. *Title: Notre Dame; **Place:** Paris, France; **Duration:** 1 hour; **Size:** 9 × 11 cm; **Tools & Materials:** watercolor and ink on paper*
Even though the artist wanted to sit as close as possible, he was unable to do so due to the amount of people walking around. But he did find a nice spot to sit down and still get a sense of perspective. He liked to sit at an angle that puts the corner directly facing him, so that he could sketch more than one side of the building.

Tips: "I like to sit at a corner where I can see more than one elevation of the architecture."

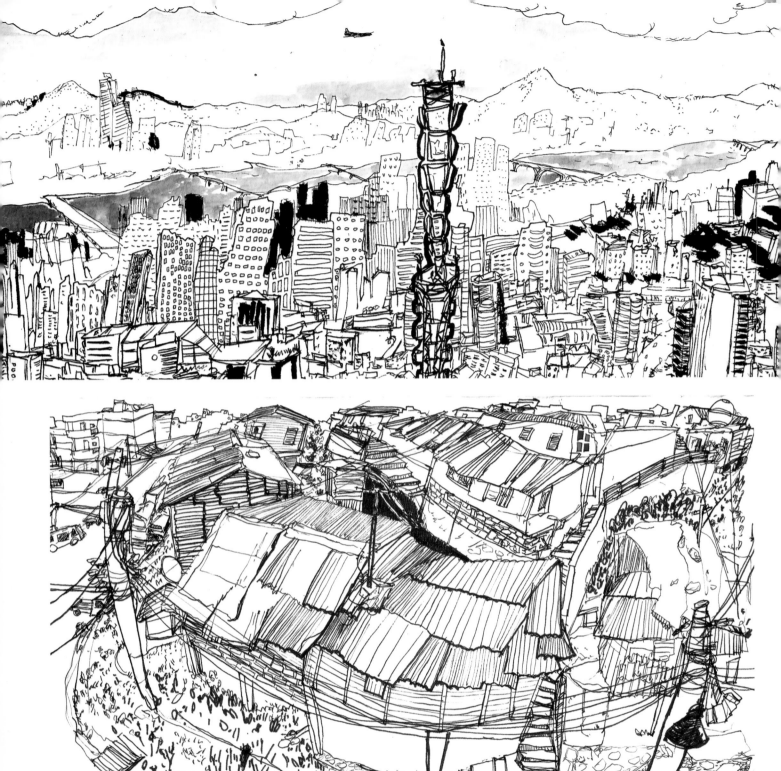

05

04. *Title:* *Forest of Buildings;* ***Place:*** *Seoul, South Korea;* ***Duration:*** *1 hour;* ***Size:*** *16 × 5 cm;* ***Tools & Materials:*** *watercolor and ink on paper*
This was one of the artist's first attempts on doing a panoramic sketch. He went up the Namsan Tower in Seoul and sketched the complex view where concrete meets the Han River.

Tips: "What I would suggest to do with a panoramic sketch (and with every other sketch, but specifically with panorama) is to start from the inside out. Start sketching an almost central reference point and let the drawing expand from there."

05. *Title:* *Bird's View of Ants;* ***Place:*** *Santo Domingo, Dominican Republic;* ***Duration:*** *1.5 hours;* ***Size:*** *10.5 × 7.5 cm;* ***Tools & Materials:*** *ink on paper/digital coloring*
There is always a certain beauty to be found while observing and sketching the metal roofs of wooden and concrete houses of hard working humans. They resemble ant colonies.

Tips: "Sometimes getting a different point of view will allow you to become one with the moment. I asked for permission to walk upstairs to the rooftop of a nearby building in La Zurza area in order to get this fantastic view. It was worth it. Trust the people and interact with them, you might get a nifty surprise."

06. *Title:* *Plaza de Santo Domingo;* ***Place:*** *Murcia, Spain;* ***Duration:*** *45 minutes;* ***Size:*** *7 × 10 cm;* ***Tools & Materials:*** *watercolor and ink on paper*
Murcia had many streets that were very similar to streets in the artist's home city, and even a tower named Santo Domingo. One of the best ways to sketch is to have a nice beverage and capture every movement within the plaza.

Tips: "I started this sketch when the plaza had very few people, but then all of a sudden, it got swarmed with people. By the time all of them got inside my composition, I didn't really leave "blank spaces" to sketch them, so I just drew on top of the already colored area."

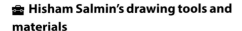
Hisham Salmin

A native of Johor, Malaysia, Hisham was born in October, 1973. Upon completing his studies, he started working in a publishing company as an illustrator and graphic designer from 1992 until 1995. He later migrated to Kuala Lumpur in 1996 and is now holding a position as art director. In 2009, he started watercolor painting in a serious manner.

Photography: Hisham Salmin

> ALTHOUGH IT IS JUST A SKETCH, MAKE SURE YOUR DRAWING IS SIMILAR TO THE REAL SUBJECT.

🧰 Hisham Salmin's drawing tools and materials

Here are the tools and materials I often use for sketching:
Paper: Bockingford, Rowney and Saunders.
Sketchbook: Monologue sketchbook and DIY sketchbook with Bockingford paper.
Pen: Pilot & Artline drawing pen, Pentel brush pen.
Pencil: Faber Castell.
Color: Schmincke Horadam watercolor tube.
Brush: Proarte Cat Tongue, Winsor & Newton squirrel mop, Mimik sets, round and flat.
Plywood board with camera bracket.
Camera easel.

✏️ Tools and materials recommended by Hisham Salmin

• Bockingford paper: Paint flows more clearly and beautifully on this paper. It doesn't dry so fast and more colors can be mixed on the paper. And cheap!
• Schmincke Horadam watercolor tube: Brilliant

and good color range. I love translucent orange and turquoise light.
• Mimik Synthetic brush set: Mimik brushes feature a revolutionary synthetic hair that accurately mimics a blend of natural squirrel and Kolinsky sable hair; they offer a wide array of popular shapes and sizes.
• Artline drawing pen: Water-based pigment ink in the Artline technical drawing pen is water-resistant and fade-proof.

👁 City in my eyes

Malaysia has a long history before independence. Once colonized by the Dutch, Portuguese, and British, it has also received influences from India and China. This led to the unique history which can be seen to this day, especially in older buildings. It has also become evident that the Malaysians of all races can live with it for a long time. I draw this history because I want to become a part of it.

01. *Title:* Sunday Morning at Jalan Gereja, Kuala Lumpur; *Place:* Kuala Lumpur, Malaysia; *Duration:* 3 hours; *Size:* 59.4 × 42 cm; *Tools & Materials:* watercolor

"Gereja" means church. Although the area is close to the church, it is full of Indians, locals or weekend travelers. It is also the location for grocery shopping.

Tips: "I am not bound by the same color in each painting. It is still fun to try the very attractive color options available in the market, especially the brand that I choose. It makes me feel free."

02. *Title:* Rest, Kampung Baru, Kuala Lumpur; *Place:* Kuala Lumpur, Malaysia; *Duration:* 2 hours; *Size:* 59.4 × 42 cm; *Tools & Materials:* watercolor

This is the only rural sight of the popular village situated in the heart of Kuala Lumpur development. The house set amidst the skyscrapers of Kuala Lumpur city centre seems to balance between quiet and busy life.

Tips: "Placing one or two human figures can add mood, size for the buildings and story-telling in a painting."

03. *Title:* Convenience Store, Jalan Tun H. S. Lee, Kuala Lumpur; *Place:* Kuala Lumpur, Malaysia; *Duration:* 3 hours; *Size:* 21 × 14.8 cm; *Tools & Materials:* ink and watercolor

This convenience store is located in a junction between Jalan Tun h.s. Lee and Jalan Sultan in Kuala Lumpur offering a variety of light consumer goods such as food, drink, and even credit for smart phones.

Tips: "Before creating a drawing, making thumbnails or simple sketches is important because you will know where the weaknesses are and what needs to be added."

04. *Title:* Old Market Square at Medan Pasar, Kuala Lumpur; *Place:* Kuala Lumpur, Malaysia; *Duration:* 2 hours; *Size:* 59.4 × 42 cm; *Tools & Materials:* watercolor

Medan Pasar is a strategic location because it is located close to several other attractions of Kuala Lumpur, such as Merdeka Square and Central Market. Besides interesting architectures, an old clock tower built in 1937 is located here.

Tips: "Not all old buildings like this are preserved. Sometimes most of them had to be demolished to make way for development. Try to sketch and take photos as long as they last."

03

04

OLD SHOP, MELAKA

05. Title: *Jalan Tunku Abdul Rahman (TAR), Kuala Lumpur;* ***Place:*** *Kuala Lumpur, Malaysia;* ***Duration:*** *3 hours;* ***Size:*** *42 × 29.7 cm;* ***Tools & Materials:*** *watercolor*

Jalan Tunku Abdul Rahman is among the most popular locations in Kuala Lumpur. As a focal point of shopping in Malaysia's multi-ethnic society, it is also close to two more popular places in KL, Dataran Merdeka and Jalan Masjid India.

Tips: "Drawing on a busy place with running vehicles and walking people not only gives you a challenge, but can be dangerous. Pick an appropriate and safe corner."

06. Title: *Corner Restaurant in Jonker Street, Malacca;* ***Place:*** *Malacca, Malaysia;* ***Duration:*** *1.5 hours;* ***Size:*** *21 × 14.8 cm;* ***Tools & Materials:*** *ink and wash*

This sketch of a restaurant on Jonker Street, Malacca, was made based on the pictures that the artist took while visiting the state. The restaurant caught his attention because of the colors of the red and green awning, adding characters to the historic city of Malacca.

Tips: "Although it is just a sketch, make sure your drawing is similar to the real subject so that it can provide an accurate view and information to anyone who sees it. Not just art."

07

08

07. *Title: Convenience Store, Jalan Doraisamy, Kuala Lumpur;* **Place:** *Kuala Lumpur, Malaysia;* **Duration:** *1.5 hours;* **Size:** *21 × 14.8 cm;* **Tools & Materials:** *ink and watercolor*

This work of art captures the calm atmosphere at Jalan Doraisamy, Kuala Lumpur. Shops began to open and newspaper delivery guy started to work. Jalan Doraisamy also caters for those who want to enjoy soup at night. They offer Tail Soup, Mutton Soup, and Tongue Soup; do not miss the Torpedo Soup (made of cow genitals).

Tips: "Quality of drawing paper used will determine the outcome of the reaction of watercolors. Good paper will certainly produce good results. However, skills and knowledge are more important."

08. *Title: Raining, Jalan Tun H. S. Lee, Kuala Lumpur;* **Place:** *Kuala Lumpur, Malaysia;* **Duration:** *1.5 hours;* **Size:** *42 × 29.7 cm;* **Tools & Materials:** *watercolor*

Quiet and slow activities in the wet season will take place as usual despite the fact that the old shop building is getting squeezed in development of Kuala Lumpur.

Tips: "I drew this during 2012. But it does not mean I'm going to keep this concept forever. Research and practice every day will make your drawing more mature and have a stronger identity."

09. *Title:* Corner Shop, Jalan Pahang, Kuala Lumpur; *Place:* Kuala Lumpur, Malaysia; *Duration:* 1.5 hours; *Size:* 42 × 29.7 cm; *Tools & Materials:* watercolor

The barber shop in this old building looks lonely, even though it is located in front of the LRT line and the busy road. The atmosphere on the weekends makes this building vacant.

Tips: "I am often asked the difference between digital and traditional paintings. Of course, each has its own specialties, but one should remember that although you can make traditional paintings become digital, the artist will always be number one in the world."

10. *Title:* Old Shop, Jalan Siu Chin, Johor Bahru; *Place:* Johor Bahru, Malaysia; *Duration:* 1.5 hours; *Size:* 59.4 × 42 cm; *Tools & Materials:* watercolor

This painting was done during a plein-air session with some friends when the artist returned to his hometown in Johor Bahru, Malaysia. An old shop that had a big tree in front is increasingly isolated in a large city.

Tips: "Drawing should be something fun. But when you are tempted to be like your idol, you will feel stressed and a loss of identity."

10

Sigrid Albert

Sigrid Albert is a professional graphic designer, and has been the principal of the Vancouver design studio StepUp Communications Inc., since 2000. She also has an art practice in drawing, and in 2010 she began drawing her neighborhood and her travel destinations, filling up sketchbooks with her favorite panorama format, both horizontal and vertical. She draws her surroundings because she has discovered a big secret that she is willing to share with everyone: once you really start looking at something, almost everything turns out to be interesting.

🧰 Sigrid Albert's drawing tools and materials

I use a sketchbook and an artist ink pen, as well as watercolors. I draw with the ink pen on location, just from looking at a scene that I've chosen, without pre-drawing anything. I prefer a horizontal sketchbook, and most of the time I use a full spread, which makes it even more horizontal; in fact, panoramic. Sometime I rotate the sketchbook and create an extremely vertical scene instead. I also like this format and it is inspired by Asian scrolls.

🖌 Tools and materials recommended by Sigrid Albert

• Sketchbook: Moleskine watercolor book: The paper is very thick and not see-through, so one can draw and paint on both sides of it.
• Pens: Pitt Artist pens: In different thicknesses from superfine to very thick, for a wide variety of lines. Pitt pens are waterproof and I can draw with them and then add watercolor on top of them without smudging the drawing.
• Watercolor: Koi watercolors: They come in a set of up to 24 decent quality colors, an integrated palette, an integrated easel, two sponges for mopping up, and a watercolor brush with a barrel to hold the water, so no water container for dipping is needed.
• Paper: Canson Montval watercolor paper: It comes in a small block of 4 × 6 inches which I can insert into the tiny easel of my Koi watercolor kit.

👁 City in my eyes

I've drawn Vancouver most frequently, since it's where I live. It is bordered by both mountains and the ocean, and it is a highly vegetated city. I find the trees that line the streets interesting, and the way some of them are pruned for overhead electrical wires; I like drawing the alleys, both residential and commercial, which run parallel to the streets of the city almost everywhere.

Photography: Sigrid Albert

01

02

> ONCE YOU REALLY START LOOKING AT SOMETHING, ALMOST EVERYTHING TURNS OUT TO BE INTERESTING.

01. Title: *View from Hotel Room at the Bellagio, Las Vegas;* **Place:** *Las Vegas, USA;* **Duration:** *1.5 hours;* **Size:** *42 × 12.7 cm;* **Tools & Materials:** *Pitt artist pen and watercolor*

The artist went to Las Vegas and stayed at the Italianate Bellagio Hotel, with a view of the fountains and the fake Eiffel Tower at the Paris Casino across the street. The Las Vegas Strip is always a surreal experience. Sigrid has never seen rain here, but on this three-day trip it rained the whole time and the skies were gray. Still, she couldn't help adding some blue to the sky.

Tips: "I used the hotel room window frame to help me with the proportions of this drawing, but did not include the frame in the drawing."

02. Title: *Plaza de la Catedral, Havana, Cuba;* **Place:** *Havana, Cuba;* **Duration:** *1.5 hours;* **Size:** *42 × 12.7 cm;* **Tools & Materials:** *Pitt artist pen and watercolor*

The artist doesn't like drawing tourist views like this one as much as drawing the more ordinary street scenes. But this square and the many covered, arched walkways in this city are spectacular, like much of Old Havana. She got to sit in the shade. The trick was to avoid drawing that whole church. She positioned herself so she could fit the tower in, but the church front is quite ornate with a lot of curved stonework, so she had most of the archway columns hidden.

Tips: "I found a shaded spot to sit because it was too hot to draw in direct sunlight. I also chose two interesting views to combine into one drawing; the view of the cathedral and plaza, and the view under the colonnades. This gives the image an expansive feeling."

03. Title: *Vancouver SeaBus Terminal and Train Tracks;* **Place:** *Vancouver, Canada;* **Duration:** *2.5 hours;* **Size:* 42 × 12.7 cm;* **Tools & Materials:** *Pitt artist pen and watercolor*

The artist sketched around the SeaBus terminal/Waterfront Station on a gorgeous, summer-like May 5th. The long bridge and passageway show people walking from downtown across the rail tracks to the SeaBus. The artist has looked at this view many times before; the cranes at the Port are some of her favorite sights ever, but she has never really looked at it as she does now. Once you really start looking at something, almost everything turns out to be interesting.

Tips: "I think shadows often add drama and definition to an urban sketch. The dark shadow under the pedestrian bridge to the SeaBus emphasizes the horizontality of the bridge's shape and gives it an almost 3-dimensional appearance."

04

04. Title: *Under Granville Bridge, Granville Island, Vancouver;* **Place:** *Vancouver, Canada;* **Duration:** *2.5 hours;* **Size:** *42 × 12.7 cm;* **Tools & Materials:** *Pitt artist pen and watercolor*

Granville Island is a great destination for locals and tourists. When the artist was drawing this work, she rotated her view about 90 degrees. For example, the view on the left side of the spread appears straight-on, and so does the view on the right side of the page, but in reality they're about 90 degrees apart. The sketchbook's panorama format, which stretches over both pages, naturally makes her do that. She just tries to keep track of the perspective as she is rotating her head.

Tips: "What you see here are straight-on views of the water and the bridge, but they are in fact at a 90-degree angle from each other. This creates a fish-eye view, which is the natural way one sees anyway. I left this drawing black and white because I wanted to achieve maximum contrast in the bridge's frame work."

05

06

07

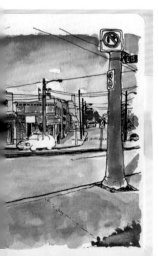

05. *Title: Kitsilano Beach Park, Vancouver;* **Place:** *Vancouver, Canada;* **Duration:** *2 hours;* **Size:** *42 × 12.7 cm;* **Tools & Materials:** *Pitt artist pen and watercolor*

This day was one of the first warmish spring days. Leaves on trees were still sparse, and it was that bright yellowish green of early spring. The artist loves spring and this work took her at least 20 minutes just to plan the drawing in her mind, calculating how to fit in all the elements she wanted, measuring the distance with her pen. She didn't do any pre-drawing because she wanted to commit to the lines the first time.

Tips: "I spent almost 20 minutes just planning out the drawing by using my pen to measure out distances. But I don't pre-draw with pencil; I just get straight to the point and draw with ink pen. I just like living with my drawing mistakes; I don't mind them."

06. *Title: Heritage Hall, Main Street, Vancouver;* **Place:** *Vancouver, Canada;* **Duration:** *1 hours;* **Size:** *42 × 12.7 cm;* **Tools & Materials:** *Pitt artist pen and watercolor*

Sketching this view, the artist had what was probably her funniest encounter yet. A man suddenly walked into her drawing, lifted up his shirt and suggested that she draw him into her sketch along with his abs, but actually it was all "belly." The artist appreciates people who make the effort to kid around, even if some jokes fall flat. One should never give up on trying to make people laugh.

Tips: "I usually bring a small folding stool to sit on, so I can pick any spot I prefer and don't have to stand for long, and I can put both my sketchbook and watercolor kit on my knees. But this time I stood, leaning against a railing. This meant I couldn't balance a watercolor kit in addition to the sketchbook, so I just left the sketch black and white."

07. *Title: The 600 Block on Kingsway, Vancouver;* **Place:** *Vancouver, Canada;* **Duration:** *2 hours;* **Size:** *42 × 12.7 cm;* **Tools & Materials:** *Pitt artist pen and watercolor*

This is one of the artist's favorite blocks on Kingsway, near the intersection with Fraser Street. The commercial establishments along Kingsway are older, and the buildings are at best functional, neither pretty nor trendy. There are, however, some signs saying things are changing in this neighborhood, and she wonders how much longer this block of buildings will remain. The location has "condo development" written all over it.

Tips: "This was a paid commission for someone who loves that block of Vancouver (I do too!). I did the drawing on one day and returned on another to add the colors. Sometimes I add color at home from photographs, but I always do the drawing on location. This is another fish-eye view."

Dai Owen

Dai has worked as a freelance illustrator based in the city of Chester, UK for over 30 years. He has a degree in Illustration from the University of Wales, and recently completed a MA in Illustration from GlyndŴr University, where he concentrated on the Reportage style of drawing.

Photography: Dai Owen

🧰 Dai Owen's drawing tools and materials

Dai always draws standing up when drawing outside, with the bottom of his sketchpad leaning on his waist. He moves about until he finds the best view to draw his subject, and this also allows him to adjust his position to check details. He does not use very expensive drawing equipment, as the standard of easily available drawing pens is now excellent.

✎ Tools and materials recommended by Dai Owen

• Main drawing pen: Uni-Pin fine line; black, water-and fade-proof, in range of sizes from 0.05 mm to 0.8 mm. I find this glides well over the paper.
• Brush Pen: Pentel brush pen; black applied through brush tip; this gives a good, deep black over an area, and can be used for quite fine work.
• Wash pen: Pentel Aquawash water brush; ready to be filled with your own prepared wash. It is useful to use your own colors; I carry two or three different washes with me.

• White pen: Pentel Hybrid gel grip pen; writes with a white gel. I use it to draw white features onto a black area.
• Paper type: Daler-Rowney Lyndhurst drawing pad; this holds cartridge paper appropriate for line and wash. I use a pad size 355 x 254 mm as this suits my preference for resting on my waist to draw.

👁 City in my eyes

Dai often sketches his home city of Chester, which is a historic tourist city with an old town wall and bridge. However, he prefers to draw the less beautiful parts, where there are contrasts between old terraces, new high-rise blocks of flats, and semi-industrial areas.

01. *Title:* *Under Hoole Bridge;* *Place:* *Chester, UK;* *Duration:* *3 hours;* *Size:* *18 × 22 cm;* *Tools & Materials:* *Uni-Pin fine line pens: 0.1, 0.5, 0.8. Pentel Hybrid gel grip pen – white.*

Downtown working areas can be interesting subjects. Here the road markings lead one into the industry and activity in the dark underbelly of the bridge and the black framed tunnel, while haphazardly parked cars become a play of shapes aided by the use of white and bold lines.

Tips: "A colored background, like the light orange one here, can bring a new feel to a drawing. This allowed me to add a brown wash for a rundown feel."

01

02. *Title: Ortigia Harbor; Place: Sicily, Italy; Duration: 2.5 hours; Size: 17 × 17 cm; Tools & Materials: Uni-Pin fine line pens - 0.1, 0.3, 0.8, Pentel brush pen (black), Pentel hybrid gel grip pen – 0.8 (white) and Daler Rowney Lyndhurst cartridge paper pad 355 × 254 mm*

The main subjects are the fishing boats in the foreground, with the town rising beyond as a stage set. The artist has paid attention to the details on the boats, seeing them as complicated and beautiful machines of the urban economy. A father and his child add a hint of recreation.

Tips: "Contrast can underline differences in a drawing. I have used black shadow areas and patterns to draw the town, while the closer harbor and boats are lighter, with fine details."

03. *Title: View from Forte Vigliena; Place: Sicily, Italy; Duration: 3 hours; Size: 18 × 21 cm; Tools & Materials: Uni-Pin fine line pens - 0.1, 0.8, Pentel brush pen (black), Pentel hybrid gel grip pen – 0.8 (white) and Daler Rowney Lyndhurst cartridge paper pad 355 × 254 mm*

The wavy line of the road, curving around the headland, is emphasized for the eye by the metal fence and parked cars. The fine-lined detail on the house front balconies speaks of age, and this is contrasted by the solid black of the buildings thrusting out from the streets behind.

Tips: "I have used a thick black line to emphasize the curving line beside the cars, which leads your eye to the block of housing – the center of the drawing."

04

05

06

07

04. Title: *Traveling Fair;* **Place:** *Chester, UK;* **Duration:** *3 hours;* **Size:** *22 × 13 cm;* **Tools & Materials:** *Uni-Pin fine line pens - 0.1, 0.3,0.5, Zig Art & Graphic Twin TUT – 803 and Daler Rowney Lyndhurst cartridge paper pad 355 × 254 mm*

This was drawn from a higher position – where one chooses to draw from is always important. The illustrator stresses the curving entry to this traveling fair by adding a tone to give a slightly 3-dimensional quality to the lorries and vans, while sideshows and the flow of people add the atmosphere.

Tips: "My addition of a brown tone transforms the feel of this drawing, by adding shadows and depth; it is important to always be aware of where shadows fall and to use them."

05. Title: *Seafront Perspective;* **Place:** *Liverpool, UK;* **Duration:** *3 hours;* **Size:** *13 × 18 cm;* **Tools & Materials:** *Uni-Pin fine line pens: 0.05, 0.1, 0.3, Pentel brush pen (black) and Daler Rowney Lyndhurst cartridge paper pad 355 × 254 mm*

This is an exercise in perspective. Clear lines define the picture and shape the sea wall, the lighthouse and rocks, and the river beyond. In addition, the strong shadows on the indented wall and buildings add a solidity and presence, and the use of a 0.05-mm pen traces the distant shoreline horizon.

Tips: "Find the right view to draw: I always spend time walking around to compare different possible views of the subject. The ideal view should fit your aims in doing the sketch."

06. Title: *Rue de l'Ecole;* **Place:** *Provence, France;* **Duration:** *45 mins;* **Size:** *17 × 24 cm;* **Tools & Materials:** *Uni-Pin fine line pens: 0.1, 0.3, 0.8, Tombo brush pen N59 and Seawhite spiral bound cartridge pad A4*

The artist drew this quite quickly, which can add a freshness to a drawing. High side walls dominate the canyon-like street with a gloomy gray-brown tone, but the viewer looks along the road to the low lighter distance and the car. The crucial point is the approaching cyclist – the drawing is her journey.

Tips: "Be ready for the unexpected drawing view to find you. In this case, I turned a corner into a side street and realized the potential of what lay before me."

07. Title: *Vicolo Sant' Anna;* **Place:** *Sicily, Italy;* **Duration:** *2 hours;* **Size:** *13 × 21 cm;* **Tools & Materials:** *Uni-Pin fine line pen – 0.1, Pentel brush pen (black), Pentel hybrid gel grip pen – 0.8 (white) and Daler Rowney Lyndhurst cartridge paper pad 355 × 254 mm*

The buildings in this narrow alleyway lean at many angles, which the artist has echoed in the outer edges. The use of solid black with white wires and pipes gives it a claustrophobic feel; this contrasts the light, uneven floor leading to the daylight and fine detail of the street beyond.

Tips: "I colored the dark, leaning walls as solid black to draw the eye into and down the alleyway, finally adding features of the buildings with a white pen."

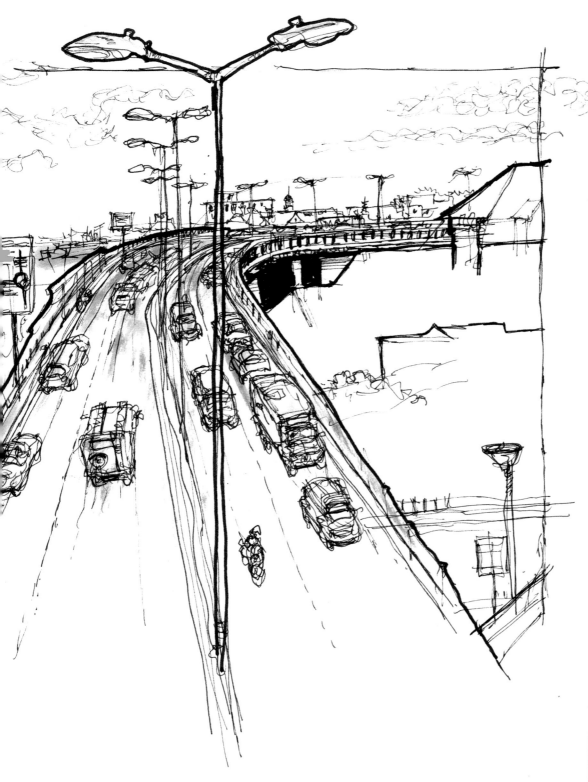

09

08. *Title:* The Rialto Bridge; *Place:* Venice, Italy; *Duration:* 2 hours; *Size:* 14 × 22 cm; *Tools & Materials:* Uni-Pin fine line pens - 0.1, 0.3,0.8 and Daler Rowney Lyndhurst cartridge paper pad 355 × 254 mm

The drawing shows the different levels of this Venetian street from the stalls in the narrow foreground, rising over the bridge to the church spire beyond. The illustrator emphasized this by drawing the walls on each side with a bold black line and having the spire burst upwards above the gap.

Tips: "I like to sketch the point which the eye is drawn to with more and finer detail than the rest; here, this is the church tower in the upper distance."

09. *Title:* Flyover; *Place:* Chester UK; *Duration:* 2.5 hours; *Size:* 22 × 22.5 cm; *Tools & Materials:* Uni-Pin fine line pens - 0.1,0.3, 0.8 and Tombo ABT N59 brush pen (gray)

Traffic and roads are part of urban life; this flyover curves through the city upon high pillars and the artist drew it looking down from a pedestrian bridge. The emerging cars are drawn in an indistinct way to imply movement, and grow larger as they speed out towards you.

Tips: "I sometimes define my drawing area with a slight, drawn rectangle based on what is to be drawn – a frame. You can also break out of this with effect."

10. *Title:* *Building Eagle's Meadow;* ***Place:*** *Wales, UK;* ***Duration:*** *2 hours;* ***Size:*** *19 × 21 cm;* ***Tools & Materials:*** *Uni-Pin fine line pens - 0.1, 0.3, 0.8 and Seawhite spiral bound cartridge pad A4*

The urban landscape is continually being renewed, and the construction involved is full of interesting detail. Here the illustrator has used the funneling entrance, with its safety fences and slope, to lead the eye in. Rising above the work site, and center stage is a tall crane, a fortunate juxtaposition.

Tips: "Horizontal surfaces like roads tend to show wear of some kind, as here the result of heavy construction traffic; I add these to my drawing to build in a visual direction."

11. *Title:* *The Old Dee Bridge;* ***Place:*** *Chester, UK;* ***Duration:*** *3.5 hours;* ***Size:*** *17 × 22 cm;* ***Tools & Materials:*** *Uni-Pin fine line pens - 0.05, 0.1, 0.3, 0.8 and Daler Rowney Lyndhurst cartridge paper pad 355 × 254 mm*

In this Christmas view the illustrator is guiding us on a journey across a historic bridge into the city, using the road markings, bridge recesses, street lamps, road angle and gateway as pointers to lead us in. The bare tree with lights and crouching figures add the feel of seasonal chill.

Tips: "I used this tree to create a strong vertical in contrast to the rest. It is also good to make a visual statement – the tree is a magnificent living presence."

12. *Title:* Seaside Kiosks; *Place:* Wales, UK; *Duration:* 2 hours; *Size:* 25.5 × 12 cm; *Tools & Materials:* Uni-Pin fine line pens: 0.05, 0.1, 0.5, Uni Posca (white) – 0.7 mm pen and light yellow card

In urban settings, people also relax. The main feature is a linear drawing of beach kiosks on a sunny background, a line that is broken by the slope of an access road. On this basic shape the artist has added a quick series of small sketches to capture the human activity.

Tips: "I drew a lot of small details in this busy seaside view, but closer examination reveals that this detail is in fact an impression. Only use what the eye needs."

13. *Title:* Terrace Backs; *Place:* Chester, UK; *Duration:* 2.5 hours; *Size:* 121× 14 cm; *Tools & Materials:* Uni-Pin fine line pens: 0.1, 0.3, 0.8, Pentel Aquawash water brush (fine) filled with own brown water color, Uni Posca (white) – 0.7 mm pen and light yellow card

The artist also looks for history and change in the suburbs. Here the focus is a terrace of older houses, seen from the back, their indented yards making a regular pattern; they are isolated and surrounded in a plain demolished world and threatened by the looming modern high-rise blocks of flats.

Tips: "The key part of the drawing is the line of terrace backs. To mark their importance I added deep shadows and a brown wash; this contrasts with the surrounding line work."

12

13

Jacek Krenz

Jacek Krenz (Ph.D., D.Sc.) is an architect and painter. He is a professor at Gdańsk University of Technology, Poland, and at University of Beira Interior in Covilhã, Portugal. He is a charter member of the Polish Watercolor Society and an instructor of the Urban Sketchers Workshop. He has written two books on architecture: *Meanings in Architecture* and *Ideograms in Architecture: Between Sign and Meaning*.

🧰 Jacek Krenz's drawing tools and materials

I most often sketch in the Leporello type of a sketchbook that I make myself. It is 15 × 21 cm, made of watercolor paper. First, I draw with water-resistant pens, and then layer over the watercolor pigments. It allows me to leave the whole sketch as light and understated as possible. I am particularly fond of watercolor painting in open air. I usually carry the basic set of 12 colors with me, two sizes of brushes, a water pen and a block of Arches rough paper 300 g, 14 × 20 inches. I like to use the landscape format, as it gives me an opportunity to widen the field of view and "follow" the scene: landscape, street, and people passing by. Such a picture becomes a sort of text, that can be read and tell a story.

✏ Tools and materials recommended by Jacek Krenz

- Moleskine watercolor sketchbooks – good quality of paper which takes watercolor strokes well while retaining texture.
- Uni-ball black pen – it is really waterproof.
- Watercolor metal box of 6 – 12 colors – convenient to carry, with an additional compartment for brush and pen.
- Arches watercolor blocks 300 g, made from 100% cotton fibre, giving strength and stability.

👁 City in my eyes

I especially like to paint old Portuguese towns, with their rich topography, narrow and often quite steep streets, with gray and rusty houses built of local stone, surrounded by orange, lemon and almond trees in bloom. The climate there makes for a longer drawing season, although sitting in the heat and burning sunshine requires a wide-brimmed hat and a good pair of dark sunglasses.

Photography: Jacek Krenz

> *A SKETCH? IT IS AN ENDLESS SPACE OF POSSIBILITIES BETWEEN SEARCHING AND FINDING ITS ESSENCE AND CHARACTERS.*

01. *Title:* *The Cathedral Square;* *Place:* *Castelo Branco, Portugal;* *Duration:* *4 hours;* *Size:* *36 × 52 cm;* *Tools & Materials:* *watercolor and Arches 300 g*
This is the main square of the old part of the city of Castelo Branco with its emblematic buildings: the School of Music and the Cathedral Igreja Matriz de São Miguel.

Tips: "When drawing architecture in parts obscured by trees, remember to make the trees partly transparent, so that the buildings remain well visible."

01

02. *Title:* *Panoramic View of Castelo Novo;* *Place:* *Castelo Novo, Portugal;* *Duration:* *1.5 hours;* *Size:* *30 × 30 cm;* *Tools & Materials:* *pen & ink with watercolor*
It depicts one of the many stone fortress towns on the Spanish-Portuguese border. It is quite an adventure to climb the steep meandering streets to get to the ruins of the castle.

Tips: "Accentuating shadows helps to visualize the tectonic structure of both urban and topographical features."

02

03. *Title:* *Panoramic View of Covilhã;*
Place: *Covilhã, Portugal;* *Duration:*
3 hours; *Size:* *48 × 24 cm;* *Tools &*
Materials: *pen & ink with watercolor*
Covilhã, an industrial city once
famous for its textiles, is situated
on a valley slope in Serra da
Estrela, the highest mountain
range in Portugal. The drawing
was made from San Antonio hill,
on the way to the university UBI,
where the artist lectures at the
Faculty of Architecture.

Tips: "Panoramic views of a city
require a lot of time, and even
more precision of line and detail.
Some parts of a view may be less
elaborate though, as in this case
the foreground."

135

04. *Title:* *The Main Square;* ***Place:*** *Constância, Portugal;* ***Duration:*** *3 hours;* ***Size:*** *36 × 22 cm;* ***Tools & Materials:*** *pen & ink with watercolor*

Cityscape of the picturesque historic town of Constância on the right bank of the River Tagus viewed from Café Vanda. By tracing different directions, the artist tried to reach beyond the classic renaissance perspective, thus inviting the observer's perception to follow multiple scenarios.

Tips: "Sometimes a classic perspective is not sufficient to depict a large and open space, such as a square or a market place. It is necessary to compress it by applying circular perspective."

05. *Title:* *Praça Rodrigues Lobo;* ***Place:*** *Leiria, Portugal;* ***Duration:*** *3 hours;* ***Size:*** *45 × 22 cm;* ***Tools & Materials:*** *pen & ink with watercolor*

This is a spring view of a square with almond trees in blossom. Similar to the drawing above in the way of compressing the perspective, the broadened view of the main square conveys an airy feeling of space organized around an ornamental mosaic of the floor.

Tips: "Not all of the scenes have to be colored and rendered to the last detail. Sometimes it is better to mark with color only the parts which we find the most important for the composition."

06. *Title:* *Streetscape;* ***Place:*** *Obidos, Portugal;* ***Duration:*** *1.5 hours;* ***Size:*** *15 × 20 cm;* ***Tools & Materials:*** *pen & ink with watercolor*

This work of art depicts a view of the cobblestoned street of a historic town surrounded by fully preserved mediaeval stone walls. Houses painted white with accents in vivid shades of blue, yellow and red give a joyous impression.

Tips: "It is advisable to base a composition on the golden ratio. Here the main accent (the red portal) is placed precisely according to this proportion."

06

JKreus 2012

07. Title: *Rua das Olarias;* ***Place:*** *Castelo Branco, Portugal;* ***Duration:*** *3 hours;* ***Size:*** *52 × 36 cm;* ***Tools & Materials:*** *watercolor and Arches 300 g*
This sketch depicts a street leading towards the Cathedral on a hot summer day, under a shadowing tree.

Tips: "Working on-site means limited time in often-changing weather conditions. Instead of 'saying it all,' it is better to focus on the main and most characteristic parts of a composition, and outline the rest in a few loose brush strokes."

SUNDAY in LUSO

BAIRO DAS ESTAÇ

OOA – 13.10.2013

08. *Title:* *A Back Street at Midday;* ***Place:*** *Luso, Portugal;* ***Duration:*** *3 hours;* ***Size:*** *15 × 20 cm;* ***Tools & Materials:*** *pen & ink with watercolor*

The picturesque small town of Luso located below the famous Bussaco Forest is renowned for its mineral spring waters. Luso is located on the hills and has many steep streets, ramps and stairs which enrich in a natural way the architectural texture.

Tips: "In a quick sketch, trees should be simplified, reduced to silhouettes by outlining just the foliage contour at their edges."

09. *Title:* *Bairro das Estacas;* ***Place:*** *Lisbon, Portugal;* ***Duration:*** *1.5 hours;* ***Size:*** *20 × 15 cm;* ***Tools & Materials:*** *pen & ink with watercolor*

This depicts a living quarter designed by architects Formosinho Sanchez and Ruy Athouguia. The human scale of this architecture is classical modernism at its best. The sketch was made during the 44 Urban Sketching Encounter organized by Urban Sketchers Portugal along Avenida de Roma famous for its 50s' architecture.

Tips: "The use of color is limited here to underline the main architectural features and to mark the shadows only."

10. *Title:* *Alfama;* ***Place:*** *Lisbon, Portugal;* ***Duration:*** *3 hours;* ***Size:*** *30 × 30 cm;* ***Tools & Materials:*** *pen & ink with watercolor*

Alfama is the oldest district of Lisbon, spreading on the slope between the São Jorge Castle and the river Tagus. The artist sketched after rain and marked reflections on the wet street surface at Rua de São Tomé marked with the tram rails. It was a challenge to draw this "fork" crossing with streets ascending and descending from the very point of their meeting.

Tips: "Painting reflections enriches the feeling of space, and adds more life to the scene."

11

11. **Title:** *View of the City from Castelo;* **Place:** *Castelo Branco, Portugal;* **Duration:** *5 hours;* **Size:** *52 × 36 cm;* **Tools & Materials:** *watercolor and Arches 300 g*

Two architectural monuments: Santa Casa de Miseric órdia and the City Museum on the left of the drawing are the initial points for the curved line of houses surrounding the City Park.

Tips: "A curve with a strong starting point recessing into the blurred distant plan provides the picture with a dynamic yet balanced rhythm of composition."

12. *Title: Streetscape; Place: Barcelona, Spain; Duration: 3 hours; Size: 41 × 26 cm; Tools & Materials: watercolor and Arches 300 g*
This work dipicts one of the narrow streets in the Barri Gòtic, Barcelona's mediaeval quarter. The perspective is formed by a sequence of diminishing lamps and the gradation of warm hues in the foreground to cold hues in the background.

Tips: "Applying air perspective by using colder and lighter shades fading into the distant space in opposition to more intense warmer shades in the foreground helps to build 3-dimensional aspect of space."

12

LARGO TRINIDADE COELHO

13

14

13. Title: *Largo Trinidade Coelho;* **Place:** *Lisbon, Portugal;* **Duration:** *3 hours;* **Size:** *36 × 13 cm;* **Tools & Materials:** *pen & ink with watercolor*

In the autumn sun, through the trees already devoid of most leaves, I could see colorful tiled façades. Inspired by the abstract transformations of the great Portuguese painter Maria Helena Vieira da Silva, this sketch crosses the border between the figurative and the abstract.

Tips: "When attempting to capture a view, it is always worth trying to discover an abstract pattern of the scene."

14. Title: *Mosteiro de Santa Maria de Alcobaça;* **Place:** *Alcobaça, Portugal;* **Duration:** *3 hours;* **Size:** *28 × 40 cm;* **Tools & Materials:** *pen & ink with watercolor*

This is a view of the northern side of the monastery drawn from a terrace of a café. A large platanus tree provides pleasantly shadowed public space in minimalistic style designed by Gonçalo Byrne.

Tips: "It is not necessary to paint all the parts of a scene in a quick sketch. Only the contour of the trees in the foreground is drawn, paint is applied between them to accentuate the impression of depth."

Tony Belobrajdic

Tony Belobrajdic was born in Rijeka, Croatia in 1958. He studied Architecture and Engineering in Croatia, then moved to New York in 1987 and since 1989 he has been living and working as a freelance illustrator in Sydney, Australia. He is a self-taught artist specialising in watercolors but also working in other media.

💼 Tony Belobrajdic's drawing tools and materials

I have tried almost every medium there is. Watercolors give me the most pleasure and often challenge me more than any other medium. With watercolors I use French Arches cold press paper and Winsor & Newton or Rembrandt paints in pans. Sometimes watercolor sketches are done on A4-sized sketching cartridge paper, just as a simple wash over pencil sketch. For paintings of larger sizes foldable easel and heavier quality paper are used.

IN ROME, INSPIRATION IS ON EVERY CORNER AND OLD DECAYING FACADES.

✏ Tools and materials recommended by Tony Belobrajdic

- Paper: French Arches cold-pressed paper, 180 gms or heavier. Cold-pressed paper, because of the rough surface, provides nice textures, especially when you are working with dry brush technique.
- Paints: Rembrandt or Winsor & Newton paints in pans. They are simpler and easier to use than tubes especially when you are painting outside the studio.
- Brushes: Large size flat brush, about two inches in size and few smaller rounded brushes. Taklon Dagger 3/8 or larger and Rembrandt Pure Sable size 10 or larger.
- Pencils: HB, B or 2B pencils.

👁 City in my eyes

When it comes to my favorite city, it must be Rome, Italy. It is my "gateway" to Europe, and whenever I can I like to spend a few days there, even when in transit. Inspiration is on every corner, as well as old decaying facades which suit my preferred limited palette choice.

Photography: Tony Belobrajdic

01. *Title:* Sydney Opera House; *Place:* Sydney, Australia; *Duration:* 30 minutes; *Size:* 30 × 21 cm; *Tools & Materials:* Yupo synthetic paper and Winsor & Newton colors

This is painted on Yupo synthetic paper. Yupo paper does not absorb paint, allowing the artist to work fast without applying too many layers of paint. It is ideal for quick watercolor sketches.

Tips: "Whites of the building structure are brought forward by the strong background and the sky behind. Form was more important than color, therefore the almost monochromatic palette."

01

02

02. *Title:* Sydney Harbor Bridge; *Place:* Sydney, Australia; *Duration:* 2 hours; *Size:* 35 × 25 cm; *Tools & Materials:* watercolor on paper, Winsor & Newton colors and Arches 300 gsm cold-pressed paper (rough)

This work depicts the bridge in late afternoon. The artist has omitted lots of details of the bridge, especially the part of the blurred North Sydney skyline in the background. He was trying to capture the atmosphere rather than reality.

Tips: "The pencil sketch was done very quickly, just showing the bridge. The rest of the painting was finished using broad, loose brush strokes just indicating forms."

04

03. Title: *Melbourne 728;* **Place:** *Melbourne, Australia;* **Duration:** *2.5 hours;* **Size:** *25 × 40 cm;* **Tools & Materials:** *watercolor on paper, Winsor & Newton colors and Arches 300 gsm cold-pressed papera and (rough)*

Maybe it's an over-dramatised ordinary busy day scene at the tram stop. The sun was behind the tram which gave the opportunity to paint people and the foreground without a great amount of detail and color.

Tips: "The perspective was accentuated by tram rails, pedestrian crossing and power lines above."

04. Title: *Somewhere in Rome;* **Place:** *Rome, Italy;* **Duration:** *45 minutes;* **Size:** *15 × 24 cm;* **Tools & Materials:** *watercolor on paper, Winsor & Newton colors and unlabelled watercolor paper (about and 100 gsm)*

The street was much wider than here on the sketch. Landscape format would be more appropriate, but the artist wanted to exaggerate diagonal shadows, so he made the street narrower and shadows deeper to add more drama to quite an ordinary scene.

Tips: "Deep shadows were the most important in this sketch. They were possibly made even longer than in the real scene."

05. Title: *Sydney from above;* **Place:** *Sydney, Australia;* **Duration:** *30 minutes;* **Size:** *25 × 18 cm;* **Tools & Materials:** *watercolor on paper, Winsor & Newton colors and unlabelled watercolor paper (about 100 and gsm)* This work was painted in 30 minutes with a "wedge-shaped" watercolor brush without a pencil sketch. The artist used this brush almost like a calligraphy pen to draw and paint with the same brush. This technique is very useful for quick sketches.

Tips: "It was done in four stages. First, shady sides of buildings; secondly, water and landscaping; third, shadows; lastly, all details which were painted using thicker and darker pigments with the tip of the brush."

06. Title: *Sydney Trams William St. c.1957;* **Place:** *Sydney, Australia;* **Duration:** *2.5 hours;* **Size:** *48 × 30 cm;* **Tools & Materials:** *watercolor on paper, Winsor & Newton colors and Canson 300 gsm cold-pressed paper.*

This is one of the series of paintings of Sydney Trams painted on Canson paper, after old, mostly black and white photographs. The artist liked the challenge of symmetrical composition and simple perspective of the scene.

Tips: "To add more interest to the painting the left side was painted with blue tones and right side with the more natural sandstone color of Sydney's streets."

07. Title: *Venice;* **Place:** *Venice, Italy;* **Duration:** *30 minutes;* **Size:** *20 × 13 cm;* **Tools & Materials:** *watercolor on paper, Winsor & Newton colors and Arches 300 gsm cold-pressed paper (rough)*
This small-sized sketch was painted in 30 minutes. It is a front on view, no perspective distortion, so strong diagonal shadows were brought forward to create a sense of depth in an otherwise very flat scene.

Tips: "Warm tones were used on the lit side of buildings and cooler blue-gray tones on the shady sides. The sky and color of water was painted very lightly."

08. Title: *Santa Maria della Salute;* **Place:** *Venice, Italy;* **Duration:** *45 minutes;* **Size:** *28 × 18 cm;* **Tools & Materials:** *watercolor on paper, Winsor & Newton colors and Canson watercolor paper (200 gsm)*
This was painted in studio after photographs. It is a quick watercolor study, painted with brush first and pencil added after. The sky, water and building details were omitted, showing only limited reflections of the buildings.

Tips: "I used tonal values to achieve greater depth. Foreground of the scene was painted in darker blue-gray tones, and distance scenery in light washed-out tones."

09. *Title:* NYC; *Place:* New York, USA;
Duration: 1 hour; *Size:* 15 × 20 cm;
Tools & Materials: watercolor on
paper, Winsor & Newton colors, Arches
300 gsm cold-pressed paper (rough)

This was painted in NY in
2009. The artist tried to keep a
limited palette in a very colorful
downtown street but still capture
typical New York tones (browns
and grays).

Tips: "Buildings' facades,
although made of many
different materials and finishes,
were painted with one tone,
giving them a look of one giant
sculpture."

09

10

11

12

10. *Title: Dubrovnik Blues; Place: Dubrovnik, Croatia; Duration: 45 minutes; Size: 26 × 18 cm; Tools & Materials: watercolor on paper, Winsor & Newton colors and Arches 300 gsm cold-pressed paper (rough)*
The artist has visited and sketched Dubrovnik many times. This one was inspired by an old photograph, where canvas awnings above shops had a deep blue color. Blue is not the typical color of Dubrovnik so this made an interesting challenge.

Tips: "I used a limited palette of red and blue tones. Accent was important on a simple one-point perspective scene."

11. *Title: Assisi; Place: Assisi, Italy; Duration: 3 hours; Size: 28 × 40 cm; Tools & Materials: watercolor on paper, Winsor & Newton colors and Arches 300 gsm cold-pressed paper (rough)*
The artist normally does smaller-sized sketches with a time limit of 30 minutes or so but this one somehow got bigger in size. At last, he tried to keep colors and tones simple and subdued.

Tips: "I was using 'negative space' by placing darker shades of volumes directly next to white parts. It creates contrast and a 3-dimensional effect."

12. *Title: Venice Canal 2009; Place: Venice, Italy; Duration: 3 hours; Size: 20 × 30 cm; Tools & Materials: watercolor on paper, Winsor & Newton colors and Arches 300 gsm cold-pressed paper (rough)*
This is a more detailed and "finished" work. It was started on site but finished in studio. Shadows were sketched together with the rest of the scene while the sun was there. For the artist that was the most important detail in this scene.

Tips: "Essentially 'Two Tones' painting. One is shadow/shade grays and the rest are warm tones of lit parts of buildings. The only color accent is the bridge in the centre of painting."

Josiah Hanchett

Josiah Hanchett was raised in several cities in Spain and Germany. He graduated in 2012 from Calvin College in Grand Rapids, Michigan with a degree in Spanish and architecture. He has worked for several years as a traveling artist and illustrator. Josiah now lives in West Orange, New Jersey and wishes to pursue a Master's Degree in Historic Preservation.

🧰 Josiah Hanchett's drawing tools and materials

I typically carry three sketchbooks with me all times: one large watercolor sketchbook, one off-white sketchbook, and one mini notebook. In my pencil case I have about five to seven pens in various sizes, a few pencils, two brush pens, three brushes, four markers, one 12-pan watercolor set, and one eraser.

✒ Tools and materials recommended by Josiah Hanchett

- Large Moleskine watercolor sketchbook. The paper is great for detailed sketches and light watercolor. They are thick enough so I'm able to draw on both sides of the page.
- Sakura Micron pen 0.05. I've used this pen ever since I started drawing three years ago. The ink dries almost instantly and doesn't bleed when I include watercolor. I like the flow of the pen and it's very fine for my detailed sketches.
- Small Koi Brush pen. The brush pen is very convenient for sketching on location. I load the pen prior to sketching so I don't have to worry about finding water everywhere I go.
- Winsor & Newton 12 pan watercolor set. The case is compact so it fits well in my small pencil case, and the watercolor set is inexpensive and will last a very long time. The colors are bold and have excellent pigment, since my drawings are so small I don't have to use too much of it.
- Grayscale Tombow Markers. The markers have two sides, one side has a large flexible brush

tip and the other is a fine tip marker for detail. I especially like the markers because they're light so they never bleed through paper.

👁 City in my eyes

New York City has such a wide range of architectural styles from many historical and cultural periods. Every neighborhood is unique, each with its own personality and distinct appeal so I like to use sketching as a way to better understand the city.

Photography: Josiah Hanchett

01. Title: *New York City Rooftops;* ***Place:*** *New York, USA;* ***Duration:*** *7 hours;* ***Size:*** *25 × 20 cm;* ***Tools & Materials:*** *Micron pens, Winsor & Newton watercolor, Koi Medium brush pen and hot-pressed Fabriano paper*

Josiah made this sketch of New York City's iconic water towers in Upper West Side. During the 19th century, New York City required all buildings that were over six stories be equipped with a rooftop water tower. Many builders made no attempt to hide the structures, making them part of the New York City skyline.

Tips: "Start sketching the basic geometric forms of the buildings and water towers and later fill in the detail."

"

SPEND SOME THINKING ABOUT HOW YOU WANT TO COMPOSE THE DRAWING BEFORE YOU START.

"

02. Title: *Chinatown Fire Escapes;* ***Place:*** *New York, USA;* ***Duration:*** *8 hours;* ***Size:*** *25 × 20 cm;* ***Tools & Materials:*** *Micron pens, Winsor & Newton watercolor, Koi Medium brush pen and hot-pressed Fabriano paper*

Josiaha made this detailed sketch of the iconic iron front buildings in Chinatown, New York City. It was a challenge drawing the shadows of the fire escapes.

Tips: "Sketch all places in the city not only what's 'beautiful.' When I do I find I'm able to appreciate it more."

03

DECEMBER 27, 2013
GUEST HOUSE ~ LIEBENZELL MISSION ~ SCHOOLEY'S MOUNTAIN

OCTOBER 13 2013
MANHATTAN SKYLINE FROM
BROOKLYN, NY

05

03. *Title:* *Manhattan Skyline;* *Place:* *New York, USA;* *Duration:* *4-5 hours;* *Size:* *42 × 13 cm;* *Tools & Materials:* *large Moleskine watercolor, Sakura Micron pens, Winsor & Newton watercolor and Koi Medium brush pen*

Josiah sketched the skyline of lower Manhattan sitting on one of the benches in Brooklyn Bridge Park, a great place to escape the city for a while. The park offers magnificent views of some of the tallest skyscrapers of the city. The artist used both pages of the spread to fit the whole skyline on the sketchbook.

Tips: "For this panoramic sketch I lightly outlined the buildings and the bridge with pencil, then used a micron pen to fill in the detail of the buildings, and later added watercolor. It helps to draw an outline in pencil first to make sure the proportions of the buildings are correct."

04. *Title:* *Liebenzell Guest House;* *Place:* *New York, USA;* *Duration:* *3 hours;* *Size:* *21 × 13 cm;* *Tools & Materials:* *large Moleskine watercolor, Sakura Micron pens, Winsor & Newton watercolor and Koi Medium brush pen*

Josiah sketched the Liebenzell Mission Guest House and headquarters in New Jersey. Sketching places of memory the artist feels he's able to relive past experiences. He grew up visiting this site throughout his childhood.

Tips: "By playing with the perspective of the building I was able to accentuate certain features of the building."

05. *Title:* *Times Square;* *Place:* *New York, USA;* *Duration:* *8 hours;* *Size:* *18 × 21 cm;* *Tools & Materials:* *Micron pens and hot-pressed Fabriano paper*

This fish-eye perspective sketch depicts one of the most chaotic intersections in the world. It's a view towards the W hotel in Times Square.

Tips: "It helps me to sketch whatever is nearest to me first and work my way to the background. In this instance, I drew the pedestrians at an eye-level horizon line first, then the taxis behind them and finished with the buildings."

JANUARY 21, 2014   HIGHLINE   NEW YORK CITY

WEDNESDAY, SEPTEMBER 18, 2013
FRONT ST.   PORT JERVIS, NY

06

06. *Title:* *Front Street Spread;* *Place:* *New York, USA;* *Duration:* *6 hours;* *Size:* *42 × 13 cm;* *Tools & Materials:* *large Moleskine watercolor, Micron pens, Winsor & Newton watercolor, Koi Medium brush pen and hot-pressed Fabriano paper*

The Front Street is a historic street of an old railroad city in Port Jervis, NY. Josiah was captivated by the street due to the amount of historic buildings. By sketching and observing them, he feels that he's able to understand the place better.

Tips: "Sketching the street with a fish-eye perspective allows me to fit more of the buildings from the street on the spread."

07. *Title:* *Highline Soldier Mural;* *Place:* *New York, USA;* *Duration:* *3 hours;* *Size:* *21 × 13 cm;* *Tools & Materials:* *large Moleskine watercolor, Micron pens, Winsor & Newton watercolor, Koi Small brush pen and Tombow brush pens*

The Soldier Mural was drawn from the High Line Park in Chelsea, New York City. The skyline has some magnificent views of the City, and this one was very intriguing.

Tips: "Be confident and focus on your drawing. However, expect people to approach you and ask questions about who you are and what you're doing. It's a great way to meet locals but will surely lengthen your drawing time."

JUNE 5, 2013
GRAND PLACE
BRUSSELS BELGIUM

08

08. *Title:* Grand Place; *Place:* Brussels, Belgium; *Duration:* 7 hours; *Size:* 30 × 21 cm; *Tools & Materials:* Micron pens, Winsor & Newton watercolor, Koi Medium brush pen and Folio Moleskine watercolor

During the summer of 2013, Josiah had the opportunity to go on a five-week trip through Europe. His goal was to capture the essence of the cities he visited through sketching, to help viewers understand the many cultures. Here he shows detail of the guildhalls in the heart of Brussels.

Tips: "Start with quick outline of the buildings with a light pencil. Don't be overwhelmed by the detail."

09. *Title:* Manhattan Bridge; *Place:* New York, USA; *Duration:* 7 hours; *Size:* 20 × 25 cm; *Tools & Materials:* Micron pens, Winsor & Newton watercolor, Koi Medium brush pen and hot-pressed Fabriano paper

This work of art depicts one of the Manhattan Bridge Towers in Brooklyn, seen here framed through nearby historic buildings. Josiah says, "This view would seem trite though it's always enchanting and a real challenge to draw."

Tips: "Spend some thinking about how you want to compose the drawing before you start."

09

J. HANCHETT '13

Trevor Dickinson

Originally from England, Trevor was trained as a printed textile designer in London and has worked with clients as diverse as the Rolling Stones, Disney and Adidas. He has also written and illustrated three children's books and painted a number of large murals in his adopted hometown of Newcastle, Australia. Trevor moved to Australia in 2002 and after a while he began to go out and stroll on the streets as a way of connecting with his environment. These drawings formed the basis for his "Newcastle Productions" project, in which he makes prints, zines, tea towels and cards as a way of spreading his vision of Australia. Since then, Trevor has added Canberra and Sydney to his body of work and continues to travel around Australia searching for more icons of day-to-day life.

Photography: Trevor Dickinson

> " IT'S HUMAN ERROR THAT GIVES THE DRAWINGS PERSONALITY! "

🧰 Trevor Dickinson's drawing tools and materials

Trevor goes out cycling with an A4 sketchbook, a stool, pens, sun cream, mosquito spray and a hat to search for good subjects to draw. Cycling allows him to get around quickly with the flexibility to stop and set up wherever he likes.

✒ Tools and materials recommended by Trevor Dickinson

• Rotring Tikky graphic pens, usually 0.5 in size. The line quality always flows strong and reliable.
• Daler Rowney or Jasart A4 150 g hardbound sketchbooks. The books feel solid and classic; the paper is thick enough to draw on both sides.
• 0.5 mechanical pencils, any brand. The pencil lines are light and loose for mapping out the pen drawings, land mechanical pencils are always sharp.
• Bifocal glasses. Unfortunately these have become a necessity when constantly focusing between close-ups and distances when drawing.
• An old dipping pen and drawing ink, any brand. It feels so good to draw a line using a scratchy unreliable ink pen. The possibilities of unfixable mistakes and drips add a danger to the process.

👁 City in my eyes

Newcastle is a working-class harbor city that has both a beautiful beach culture and a gritty urban decay reflecting the old steelworks that once thrived. It's also Australia's second oldest city, so there's plenty of Victorian architecture alongside classic Australian weatherboard. There are so many different aspects to draw and the perfect climate to go out all year round.

01. Title: *Albert Street Uniting Church;* **Place:** *Brisbane, Australia;* **Duration:** *3.5 hours;* **Size:** *42 × 29.7 cm;* **Tools & Materials:** *graphic pen and sketchbook*
The artist drew this because he liked all the tall buildings surrounding the cute church. The church is actually very neat and well presented, but he has made it loom a bit worn out and rough – not on purpose though!

He doesn't think he'll ever reach the point of drawing perfectly proportioned architecture; he likes how scrappy his drawings look.

Tips: "A lot of time is spent counting bricks, windows and weatherboards. If they don't all fit in the space I draw less of them."

02. Title: *Fred Ash Building;* **Place:** *Newcastle, Australia;* **Duration:** *3 hours;* **Size:** *21 × 29.7 cm;* **Tools & Materials:** *graphic pen and sketchbook*
This is an early morning view of the Visitor Information Centre, which was drawn with the intention of getting them to stock his Newcastle zines and cards. After drawing it he found out that they were about to close down so the plan didn't pan out. He still likes the drawing though.

Tips: "When shading with pen, I use lines and cross hatching to give an object body and shape."

03. *Title:* Manuka Pool Canberra; *Place:* Canberra, Australia; *Duration:* 3 hours; *Size:* 21 × 29.7 cm; *Tools & Materials:* ink and brush and digital color

This is an old established pool in Canberra. It hasn't changed much since it was built. It was on the artist's list of things to draw for a while. What finally motivated him to draw it was the installation of the giant fly swatters in the sports ground behind the pool.

Tips: "I always photograph a scene I draw in case I'll need it for color reference later. Sometimes I go back to photograph on different days if the colors aren't quite strong enough."

04. *Title:* Sirius Apartments Sydney Harbor; *Place:* Sydney, Australia; *Duration:* 3 hours; *Size:* 42 × 29.7 cm; *Tools & Materials:* graphic pen and sketchbook

This artist drew this while standing on Sydney Harbor Bridge. It was a hot, loud and very uncomfortable three hours. The Sirius apartments must be among the best located government housing in the world and they make quite a brutal impact on the approach to Sydney.

Tips: "Photographing the scene also helps if I need to finish a drawing at home. It helps when there isn't enough time or light to continue on site."

05. Title: *Derelict Fruit and Veg store;* **Place:** *Newcastle, Australia;* **Duration:** *3 hours;* **Size:** *21 × 29.7 cm;* **Tools & Materials:** *graphic pen and sketchbook*

This fruit and veg shop has become increasingly shabby since it closed down a year or two before the artist drew this picture. It stands on a main traffic route on the way to the city; a lot of Newcastle locals know it. When drawing this the artist was so relaxed that he ended up having a nap on the street, and that's probably why the line work is looser than usual. He once fell asleep drawing the Parliament House, Canberra. There aren't many countries where you can sit and have a nap 15 meters from the seat of the Parliament and not get disturbed.

Tips: "A benefit from drawing with pen is that it's impossible to rub out, so all mistakes have to be kept; it's this human error that gives the drawings personality."

06. Title: *Storage King Adamstown;* **Place:** *Newcastle, Australia;* **Duration:** *2 hours;* **Size:** *29.7 × 21 cm;* **Tools & Materials:** *pencil and sketchbook*

The artist drew a classic tin-roofed warehouse found at the bottom of a typical Australian street. Corrugated iron is one of the most popular building materials in Australia, and it's everywhere. He drew this purely because of the painted tin roof. To be in this building during an Aussie rainstorm day would be something to hear.

Tips: "This one was drawn with a mechanical pencil. I like the consistent clean lines they give. Usually a 2B 0.5 is my choice."

06

07

07. *Title:* The Pump House Carrington; *Place:* Newcastle, Australia; *Duration:* 2 hours; *Size:* 29.7 × 21 cm; *Tools & Materials:* graphic pen and sketchbook

The Pump House is a derelict Newcastle building in an industrial area near the harbor. This drawing went quite wonky but as ever the artist tried to keep calm and carry on. He regrets taking a shortcut by crisis crossing the lines on the right of the fence; the left hand side captures the fence better as he followed the line of the wire.

Tips: "The building and fence don't quite touch the post. I do this to separate the foreground from the background."

08

09

08. Title: *Botanic Gardens Adelaide;* **Place:** *Adelaide, Australia;* **Duration:** *2.5 hours;* **Size:** *29.7 × 21 cm;* **Tools & Materials:** *graphic pen*

The artist spent four days wandering around Adelaide looking for subjects to draw. With a sketchbook there's no reason to be bored. It's also the closest way he gets to meditate and live in the moment.

Tips: "A benefit of using pens is that the drawings look great when they are reduced in size. I make zines of my drawings and this technique gives beautiful scans and copies."

09. Title: *Newcastle Resistance Centre;* **Place:** *Newcastle, Australia;* **Duration:** *2 hours;* **Size:** *21 × 29.7 cm;* **Tools & Materials:** *graphic pen and sketchbook*

This building is in the middle of the wedding shop area of Newcastle; the building is short and shouts with slogans. "Save the figs" refers to protests against the removal of fig trees from the front of Newcastle Art Gallery, which was a local news story that carried on for weeks. The artist likes the moment in time that this drawing captures. At the same time the building calls for us to occupy the Wall Street; he is not sure if any Newcastle locals made the trip to New York to do as requested.

Tips: "Sometimes I am commissioned to draw a specific building. To find out the time of day for the best light I use a phone app called Sun Seeker that plots the course of the sun on a map."

10. Title: *Icebergs Bondi Sydney;* **Place:** *Sydney, Australia;* **Duration:** *3 hours;* **Size:** *29.7 × 42 cm;* **Tools & Materials:** *graphic pen*

The artist was mainly interested in the color of the pools against the color of the ocean. He usually draws with a plan to color the images at a later date. The viewpoint to draw this subject is quite limited though the artist tried to get a drawing of the whole building. If he had gone for a lower angle to show the whole building, he would have lost the pools.

Tips: "I use a 38 × 9 cm drawing board clipped to my sketchbook to keep it rigid. It's made out of light corflute and fits into a bag easily."

Sofia Pereira

Sofia Pereira is a Portuguese designer and illustrator who loves sketching and painting. She studied in the Faculty of Fine Arts of the University of Lisbon, and has a degree in Communication Design. She now works as a freelancer and sketches as a hobby. She uses her sketchbook as a way to express and capture the moment, and takes her daily events as an inspiration. Sofia hopes to keep visiting new places, learning new things, and carry on representing the world in her own way. For more information about Sofia, please visit www.behance.net/asofiap.

🧰 Sofia Pereira's drawing tools and materials

I usually take my daily events as an inspiration for my work, and for that I need to be prepared – I take some pencils with me, a box of watercolors and a sketchbook. Then I just need an opportunity to draw. To start off, most often I will use a pencil or pen to sketch the outlines, and after I will color the work with watercolors or ink. The most important thing is to have fun at your own rhythm.

🖌 Tools and materials recommended by Sofia Pereira

- Colored pencils: Most preferred brands – Derwent, Caran d'Ache, and Faber Castle. They are of good quality and have several types of pencils from watercolor to pastel.
- Watercolors: I use Van Gogh watercolors, because they are of great quality and don't ruin your budget.
- Indian ink: You can get it from art supply stores. I use the Chinese ones with no brand. A little goes a really long way with this bottle. As long as you have a small container, you can carry a small amount of the ink with you wherever you go.
- Ecolines: Winsor & Newton ones are great to add a bit of color to a piece.
- Permanent Ink pens: Most preferred brands – Uni Pin fine Line (Water and Fade Pigment Ink) in 0.05, 0.1 and 0.3 mm. Staedtler Triplus Fineliner (Dry Safe) in 0.3 mm. These are great and if you're using wet materials on top of it, they won't smudge.

👁 City in my eyes

Drawing is a relaxing therapy: It clears my mind and makes me happy. The natural landscapes and beaches I love to draw in the south of Portugal really complement that feeling. Nevertheless, if I had to pick an urban landscape I've already drawn, it would probably be in Poland – I was really fascinated by the tidy and colorful squares there.

DRAWING IS A RELAXING THERAPY: IT CLEARS MY MIND AND MAKES ME HAPPY.

Photography: Sofia Pereira

01. *Title: Praha; Place: Prague, Czech Republic; Duration: 30 minutes; Size: 25 × 20 cm; Tools & Materials: watercolors and pen*

What fascinated the artist most in this city are the colors, the details, and the perfection of the buildings. Everything looks like a monument worth seeing, or a painting worth a frame.

Tips: "When something stands out in a landscape, you can always highlight it even more in your drawing."

STACJA RYNEK

RESTAURANT & BAR STACJA RYNEK

02. *Title:* *Warsaw;* ***Place:*** *Warsaw, Poland;* ***Duration:*** *1 hour;* ***Size:*** *29.7 × 21 cm;* ***Tools & Materials:*** *watercolors and Indian ink*

"Rynek Starego Miasta" (Old Town Market Place) is a colorful and lively square in Warsaw. Each building has its own color, and it looks like Lego houses all placed together. There's something really special about this place.

Tips: "Drawing is about having fun. It doesn't need to be realistic or make sense. Make sure you break the rules and make things your own way."

03. *Title:* *Blue Mosque;* ***Place:*** *Istanbul, Turkey;* ***Duration:*** *30 minutes;* ***Size:*** *21 × 14.8 cm;* ***Tools & Materials:*** *watercolors and Indian ink*

Even though part of this city is still in Europe's territory, we can really feel the cultural differences, just by looking to the architecture of these buildings. This Mosque sits in front of the well-known Hagia Sophia. They are monumental and ostentatious buildings, a real "Turkish delight." Despite the obvious cultural contrast with the major part of Europe the artist really felt at home, as she found many similarities to Portugal in this city.

Tips: "Distortion and perspective can help you fit whatever you're drawing inside the sketchbook limits."

04. *Title:* *St. Basil's Cathedral;* ***Place:*** *Moscow, Russia;* ***Duration:*** *50 minutes;* ***Size:*** *21 × 14.8 cm;* ***Tools & Materials:*** *watercolors and pen*

No doubt this is one of the most awesome buildings in Europe. The colors and the shapes are incredible, and they seem to be taken from some sort of fantasy tale. As people travel through Russia they get to see a lot of these domes, but this one has some special and vibrant colors to it. The artist couldn't pass up drawing this wonder that lights up the Red Square

Tips: "When sketching you don't need to worry about perfectionism or mistakes, because that's a part of the process, and that's one of the things that will make your drawing unique."

05. *Title: Barco Rabelo; Place: Oporto, Portugal; Duration: 40 minutes; Size: 14.4 × 10.5 cm; Tools & Materials: watercolors, Indian ink and pen*

This drawing was made on the Southern side of the Douro River, where we can see many emblematic icons of this region. "Barco Rabelo" is a typical boat that for centuries was used to carry people and pipes of Port Wine along the Douro River. In the background, there is the D. Luis Bridge, a metal arch bridge that connects Oporto and Vila Nova de Gaia.

Tips: "Regarding perspective, it's always a good tip to use darker and richer strokes on what is closer. Having multiple layers will add depth to the drawing."

06. *Title: London; Place: London, England; Duration: 20 minutes; Size: 14.4 × 10.5 cm; Tools & Materials: watercolor and pen*

Piccadilly Circus is an intersection full of lights and people. Even if it's cold, it is really worth it to come to this place at night and just take a look to see all the life around us. The unique contrast of the monochromatic buildings with the constant red color, whether it is a bus or just a telephone post, really stands out throughout the whole city.

Tips: "Using a pen to draw the outlines is a good and quick way to capture the moment without taking too much time. It will work as a guideline, and you can always add something more afterwards."

05

06

07

08

Rua Augusta is a street in the heart of Lisbon's downtown. This drawing represents the view from the top of the Arch, where we can see, on one side, all the city, and on the other the Tagus River. The pattern of the "Calçada Portuguesa," the iconic Portuguese mosaic pavements, dresses the floors of these streets, creating a sort of tapestry effect when seen from the top.

Tips: "Perspective is important. Try to find the best angle before starting your drawing."

This was drawn in a small town the artist frequently visits, in the southwestern part of Spain, during a very sunny Siesta time. Due to the time zone difference the artist always gets there one hour late. You are able to "hear" a really comforting and calming silence in the streets during lunch time while everyone is sleeping, which provides a great opportunity to sit back and do a quick drawing.

Tips: "Feel free to mix your materials. Having different textures and colors can create some unexpected results."

Benedetta Dossi

Benedetta Dossi came to Rome from Trieste in 2006 and practiced concept design for four years in Rainbow CGI animation studio. She attended comic schools in Milan and Rome, before the course of artistic studies in Trieste. For more information about Benedetta, please visit www.365onroad. blogspot.it.

🧰 Benedetta Dossi's drawing tools and materials

The first thing to do is to experiment with a lot of materials and find the most congenial and the one with which we feel most comfortable. There is a close relationship between the person, style, and type of material used. There are some artists who love sketching in pencil; someone else might prefer to practice directly in watercolor. I prefer to draw directly in ballpoint pens and sometimes add some strokes of color.

✏ Tools and materials recommended by Benedetta Dossi

- Ballpoint pen: a simple Bic. This is the material I use for the base. I prefer this instrument because it allows me to create a fast and dynamic line.
- Watercolor: Winsor & Newton. I have the portable version; it is very useful if you want to add some brush strokes in few minutes.
- Colored pencil: I use every brand, from the children's pencils (Giotto, Faber-Castell) to the professional instruments (Caran d'Ache).
- Brush: The brand I used more, for this item, is the Winsor & Newton brushes.

👁 City in my eyes

Rome is the city that I draw the most. I used to say that nine lives would not be enough to portray this historic city. It is an open museum where the different styles of architecture are overlapped in centuries. Close to a Roman arch you can find a modern palace, an early Christian church with a 16th century facade, a legendary fountain, or an ancient 19th century café.

Photography: Marco Dossi

I PREFER TO DRAW DIRECTLY IN BALLPOINT PENS AND SOMETIMES ADD SOME STROKES OF COLOR.

01

01. Title: *Garbatella;* **Place:** *Rome, Italy;* **Duration:** *30 minutes;* **Size:** *30 x 21 cm;* **Tools & Materials:** *ballpoint pen, watercolor and Moleskine sketchbook* Garbatella is a typical and popular district in Rome. This highway view is an illusion. The artist was drawing sitting in a tripod at ground level. She loves using perspectives to modify the point of view and imagine herself flying over the structures.

Tips: "If you want to create a distortion, the best way I find is to identify the main lines of your subject and sketch them slightly on the notebook, bringing them to the same focus point. Then you can draw the others, secondary lines, that will be consistent to the first guide lines."

02. *Title:* Tour in Bologna, Piazza Santo Stefano; *Place:* Bologna, Italy; *Duration:* 40 minutes; *Size:* 35 x 25 cm; *Tools & Materials:* ballpoint pen and Moleskine sketchbook

On a sunny afternoon, Benedetta and her brother sketched this little square in Bologna. It's a great idea to draw with other people because you can compare the different styles, views and techniques originated by the same subject.

Tips: "Before starting to color, I prepared the main colors and the main shades. One is tending toward a blue\violet\dark tone, and the other toward a yellow\orange\light tone (used for the illuminated part)."

03. *Title:* Il Duomo; *Place:* Florence, Italy; *Duration:* 40 minutes; *Size:* 26 x 21 cm; *Tools & Materials:* ballpoint pen

Benedetta spent 40 minutes sketching this drawing. Her focus here was to create the illusion of details, adding a lot of fine points in certain parts. The difficulty was to keep in mind the sense of the perspective while concentrating on one single column, statue, or decoration.

Tips: "If you have to sketch a detailed architecture, the best trick I can suggest to you is don't sketch everything, but only the lines that can give the impression of the volume. The art of design is closely connected to the theme of symbols; you have to give only an impression of the shapes."

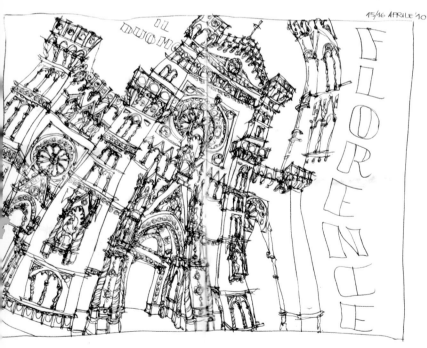

Stefano

FORO ROMANO

04

degli ASinelli

05

04. *Title:* Foro Romano; *Place:* Rome, Italy; *Duration:* 40 minutes; *Size: 26 x 21 cm; Tools & Materials:* ballpoint pen, watercolor and Moleskine sketchbook

This sketch is slightly outside the box in comparison to Benedetta's tendency to deform the architecture in a more dynamic shape. Here the structures are more monumental and the colors tend to be of a gray tone, giving a sense of historical atmosphere and a sense of volume.

Tips: "When I choose the tones I like to use some blue\violet colors for the shadow area, and a yellow\light green color for the illuminated area, because these tones give me a sense of breathing the atmosphere."

05. *Title:* Tour in Bologna, La Torre degli Asinelli; *Place:* Bologna, Italy; *Duration:* 20 minutes; *Size: 35 x 25 cm; Tools & Materials:* ballpoint pen and Moleskine sketchbook

In this sketch, Benedetta drew an high-view of Bologna. The challenge was to create a sense of dynamic, living white spaces, and focus on the details only in a few parts. It seems bizarre, but the biggest difficulty was to restrain herself from drawing all over the page.

Tips: "Sometimes, while you're sketching a panorama rich in details, you may be forced to leave some suggestions of a shape rather than drawing the whole. This allows you to draw faster and to give a lightness to the drawing."

06. *Title:* *The Canals of Venice;* ***Place:*** *Venice, Italy;* ***Duration:*** *40 minutes;* ***Size:*** *36 x 25 cm;* ***Tools & Materials:*** *ballpoint pen, watercolor and Moleskine sketchbook*

In this sketch Benedetta wanted to give a sense of lightness with the watercolors, choosing delicate tones and a sense of refinement to create the illusion of details by focusing on the black details in definite areas.

Tips: "Some cities inspire particular tones. Before adding the watercolor, try to feel what sensations give you the feel of the panorama; some feelings will be related to specific colors."

07. *Title:* *Rome in March;* ***Place:*** *Rome, Italy;* ***Duration:*** *20 minutes;* ***Size:*** *36 x 25 cm;* ***Tools & Materials:*** *ballpoint pen, watercolor and Moleskine sketchbook*

On this occasion Benedetta was sketching with another urban sketcher. It is always an opportunity for growth for her to compare her style with other styles and techniques. You realize increasingly how much more important the personal expression is, rather than executing a good technical drawing. The focus here was to transform a static structure into a dynamic, dancing shape.

Tips: "Using the watercolor doesn't always mean creating a beautiful detailed canvas full of colors; you can choose a part of the sketch where you want to focus the attention, and add only some fast strokes. The contrast between the black and white and the watercolor part creates a good result."

07

Francine Bidal-St-Aubin

Francine Bidal-St-Aubin is a nurse clinician who has worked in community health for over 30 years. For as far back as she can remember, the artist has always had a project to work on, from stained glass to oil painting and most recently sketching. Through sketching she is able to appreciate Montreal in a whole new light. Having recently moved closer to the downtown core, she is looking forward to riding her bike to different areas and sketching them, one building at a time. She enjoys the social aspect of belonging to a sketching group and sharing her work with other artists all over the world.

Francine Bidal-St-Aubin's drawing tools and materials

I try to combine cycling and sketching as much as I can. My bicycle is equipped with two side saddle bags. One bag carries all my sketching tools such as my sable brushes, cold-pressed block, and a plastic traveling paint tray. The other bag is for my lunch and water.

Tools and materials recommended by Francine Bidal-St-Aubin

- Fabre Castle waterproof pen kit: I like to use pens of different sizes so that thinner or thicker lines can give some dimension to my drawings.
- Dollorama 12 inch tripod seat: This inexpensive seat fits in my saddle bag and can be used if there are no ledges or benches to sit on.
- Windsor & Newton sable brushes: When researching sketching tools a wise tip led me to purchase the best brushes in different sizes. They hold a large quantity of paint and water.
- Block cold-pressed 140 lb watercolor paper: I like to work with blocks of paper as it keeps the paper from rippling when it dries. Using sheets of paper as opposed to a sketchbook permits me to return and offer my sketches to the owner of the building.

City in my eyes

Montreal is a remarkable city with an eclectic flair of old and new architecture. The varieties of buildings include elevators, warehouses, mills, refineries, heritage sites, modern skyscrapers, churches, and cathedrals. It is no wonder that sketching subjects are endless in this friendly and safe city.

MONTREAL IS A SKETCHER'S PARADISE, OFFERING A WIDE RANGE OF ARCHITECTURAL DESIGN!

Photography: Francine Bidal-St-Aubin

01

01. **Title:** *Room With a View;* **Place:** *Quebec, Canada;* **Duration:** *5 hours;* **Size:** *12 × 9 cm;*
Tools & Materials: *HB pencil, Fabre Castel ecco pigment permanent pen size 0.4 and 0.6, Holbein and Van Gogh tube watercolor paint, Canson cold press 140 lb paper and Winsor & Newton sable watercolor brushes sizes 3, 4, 6 & 8.*
Griffintown, founded in 1820, was mainly populated by Irish immigrants. In 2011, new condos were built inside century-old buildings. The artist sketched from her son's seventh floor condo. What captured her attention was how much green space was preserved in the downtown core.

Tips: "Use the 'thumb and pencil' method of measuring lengths and determine the angles of whatever you are trying to draw."

02

03

02. Title: *Old Montreal Skyline;* **Place:** *Quebec, Canada;* **Duration:** *3 hours;* **Size:** *14 × 10 cm;* **Tools & Materials:** *HB pencil, Fabre Castel ecco pigment permanent pen size 0.4 and 0.6, Holbein and Van Gogh tube watercolor paint, Arches 140 lb paper and Winsor & Newton sable watercolor brushes sizes 3, 4, 6 & 8*
When driving into Montreal from the South Shore, the artist finds the view spectacular. Height restrictions due to the nearby Mount Royal keeps buildings from being as tall as in other major cities. She loves sketching the waterfront where the 18th- and 19th-century buildings have been retained.

Tips: "Get the horizontal line in first, remembering the 1/3 rule. Then work from one side of the paper to the other and then foreground to background."

03. Title: *Meldrum Allied Van Lines Moving Company;* **Place:** *Quebec, Canada;* **Duration:** *6 hours;* **Size:** *9 × 12 cm;* **Tools & Materials:** *HB pencil, Fabre Castel ecco pigment permanent pen size 0.4 and 0.6, Holbein and Van Gogh tube watercolor paint, Arches cold press 100% cotton 140 lb paper and Winsor & Newton sable watercolor brushes sizes 3, 4, 6 & 8*
This moving company has been family-owned for more than 75 years. It specializes in long distance moves and storage. What attracted the artist to this building was the unique angles and brickwork. It took several of her lunch breaks to complete this sketch.

Tips: "Drawing is at least 50% observation. If you want to do a detailed sketch you really have to study it."

04. Title: *Optometry Clinic of Ste-Anne-de-Bellevue;* **Place:** *Quebec, Canada;* **Duration:** *4 hours;* **Size:** *10 × 14 cm;* **Tools & Materials:** *HB pencil, Fabre Castel ecco pigment permanent pen size 0.4 and 0.6, Holbein and Van Gogh tube watercolor paint, Arches cold press 100% cotton 140 lb paper and Winsor & Newton sable watercolor brushes sizes 3, 4, 6 & 8*

Ste-Anne-de-Bellevue, an on-island suburb, was founded in 1703. The artist often combines cycling and sketching in this peaceful area. If weather permits, she stops to sketch the older buildings that have been converted into businesses or restaurants. What attracted her to this building was the uniqueness of the brickwork.

Tips: "Try to find a comfortable bench to sit when doing a detailed sketch, as you can be there for several hours. Keep a hat and sunscreen in your bag for those sunny sketching days."

05. Title: *Rue Somerled;* **Place:** *Quebec, Canada;* **Duration:** *2.5 hours;* **Size:** *8.5 × 5.5 cm;* **Tools & Materials:** *HB pencil, Fabre Castel ecco pigment permanent pen size 0.4 and 0.6, Holbein and Van Gogh tube watercolor paint, Arches 140 lb paper and Winsor & Newton sable watercolor brushes sizes 3, 4, 6 & 8*

The construction of St-Joseph Oratory began in 1934 and ended in 1967. This imposing structure is perched on Mount Royal and can be seen from many parts of Montreal. The artist sketched on Somerled Street where you can see this majestic architecture appearing over the trees.

Tips: "When drawing a street, start with simple contours with a pencil, and then add the details with a watercolor ink pen. I usually start by drawing in the road and work from one side to the other."

04

05

06. Title: *Christ Church Cathedral;* ***Place:*** *Quebec, Canada;* ***Duration:*** *5 hours;* ***Size:*** *10 × 14 cm;* ***Tools & Materials:*** *HB pencil, Fabre Castel ecco pigment permanent pen size 0.4 and 0.6, Holbein and Van Gogh tube watercolor paint, Arches cold press 100% cotton 140 lb paper and Winsor & Newton sable watercolor brushes sizes 3, 4, 6 & 8*

What the artist loves about Montreal is the conservation of century-old structures. Christ Church Cathedral, a Neo-Gothic design, was built from 1822 to 1856. In 1987 this church was supported on stilts while an underground mall and a 34-floor sky scraper were being built.

Tips: "A common drawing mistake is finding out the sketch does not fit onto the paper. A great way to get your drawing to fit is to find some of the major points such as the top or a steeple or a corner of a building, and plot these onto your paper with dots."

07. Title: *Chinese Pavillion Montreal Botanical Garden;* ***Place:*** *Quebec, Canada;* ***Duration:*** *1 hour;* ***Size:*** *9 × 7.5 cm;* ***Tools & Materials:*** *HB pencil, Fabre Castel ecco pigment permanent pen size 0.4 and 0.6, Holbein and Van Gogh tube watercolor paint, Arches cold press 100% cotton 140 lb paper and Winsor & Newton sable watercolor brushes sizes 3, 4, 6 & 8*

Montreal Botanical Gardens, founded in 1931, covers 185 acres and boasts more than 22,000 species of plants and 31 specialized gardens. The artist enjoys peaceful places to sketch, and this place does not disappoint. She plans to sketch here this fall during the Magical Chinese Lantern Festival.

Tips: "Try different styles when sketching, adjust them to your particular mood that day or to the subject you are observing. Just be consistent within your sketch. For example if you start your sketch loose and gestural, keep the entire sketch that way to ensure that it is unified and harmonious."

Bidah

08. *Title:* Lachine Canal; *Place:* Quebec, Canada; *Duration:* 3 hours; *Size:* 10 × 14 cm; *Tools & Materials:* HB pencil, Fabre Castel ecco pigment permanent pen size 0.4 and 0.6, Holbein and Van Gogh tube watercolor paint, Arches cold press 100% cotton 140 lb paper and Winsor & Newton sable watercolor brushes sizes 3, 4, 6 & 8, and natural sponge.

The Lachine Canal is a 15-km canal passing through the southwestern part of the city. It has been designated as a National Historical Site of Canada. The artist is often seen biking on the canal's bike path searching for her next sketching location.

Tips: "Sometimes it isn't easy to decide what to sketch. Vast panoramas and landscapes can be overwhelming. Cropping the scene with your hands or a viewfinder helps to solve this problem. Many examples of viewfinders can be found online."

09. *Title:* Avenue du Musée; *Place:* Quebec, Canada; *Duration:* 2.5 hours; *Size:* 5.5 × 8.5 cm; *Tools & Materials:* HB pencil, Fabre Castel ecco pigment permanent pen size 0.4 and 0.6, Holbein and Van Gogh tube watercolor paint, Arches cold press 100% cotton 140 lb paper and Winsor & Newton sable watercolor brushes sizes 3, 4, 6 & 8.

Avenue du Musée was renamed in 1975 due to the presence of the Montreal Museum of Fine Arts. The artist sketched the street from the museum window during an urban sketcher outing. It's a great location to sketch during the cold winter months.

Tips: "In the cold winter months, sketch inside public buildings such as museums, courthouses, libraries or cafés."

Roger De Muth

Roger De Muth is an award-winning designer, illustrator, photographer, and gardener. His work has won Merit Awards from the Society of Illustrators in New York and the American Institute of Graphic Arts in Los Angeles, and has been seen in the *New York Times*, *American Illustration*, *Nobrow Magazine* in London, and the *Design Journal*, published in Seoul, South Korea. Roger De Muth is currently a professor of Illustration at Syracuse University (since 1979) and is the Creative Director of De Muth Design (since 1970). He has wanted to be an artist since he was five years old. For more information about Roger, please visit www.behance.net/rogerdemuth.

Photography: Roger De Muth

IT'S IMPORTANT TO USE THE BEST MATERIALS YOU CAN AFFORD.

🧰 Roger De Muth's drawing tools and materials

I love the materials I use in my work. I use Arches hot or cold-pressed watercolor paper 300 lb, an old dip style pen with Sepia Ink, and Winsor & Newton Watercolors. It's important to use the best materials you can afford. It pays off.

✒ Tools and materials recommended by Roger De Muth

• Winsor & Newton watercolor: I prefer Winsor & Newton as they've stood the test of time. They are finely ground, and lightfast.
• Natural hair sable brushes: I use many brands of brushes but love the Winsor & Newton Series 7 with a beautiful point. Even while using a large brush, you can do detailed work.
• Esterbrook dip Pen: I have a large collection of Esterbrook 757 School Medium Oval dip pens. I buy them on eBay. The pens have a small, ball-like feature, and it glides over the surface of the rough watercolor paper.
• Waterproof Higgins India Ink: Higgins inks are lightfast and waterproof. Once the sketch is done, I ink the drawing, and color it in. The ink doesn't smear because it contains shellac.

👁 City in my eyes

I am currently working on "My Italian Sketchbook," a series of several hundred watercolor paintings of Italy. I have been working on it for a couple of years, and it's almost finished. Italy is a beautiful country to draw and paint, as it's so interesting. It's ancient and filled with beautiful classical architecture. The food is pretty good, too! I've spent time in Rome, Venice, Riomaggiore, Lucca, Vicenza, Naples, Amalfi, Florence, and Pompei. So much to see, so little time.

01

01. *Title:* *Petrossian Restaurant;* *Place:* *New York, USA;*
Duration: *7 days;* *Size:* *21 × 21 inches;* *Tools & Materials:* *ink,*
pencil and watercolors
One of the artist's favorite buildings in New York,
the Alwyn Court Building has an amazing facade.
It's built of terra cotta and limestone and filled with
detail over the entire building. It's one of the most
decorative buildings in New York. This painting was
selected for the 55th Annual Exhibition at the Society
of Illustrators in NY.

Tips: "This painting took about
a week. It's loaded with detail,
and involved lots of patience. The
inking took me about four days
and the same with the sketch.
The painting part took about two
days."

02. Title: *South Street Market;* ***Place:***
Philadelphia, USA; ***Duration:*** *1
week;* ***Size:*** *20.5 × 16 inches;* ***Tools &
Materials:*** *ink, pencil and watercolors*
The South Street in Philly is a
pretty interesting place, and the
heart of the "Magic Garden"
section of the city. An artist has
transformed many buildings
with his mosaics, and mirrors.
It's worth a trip just to see it.
Roger really liked working on
this painting as it had all the right
elements. It's a slightly run-down
Victorian building with a Mansard
roof, a moody atmosphere and
with a single solitary figure.

Tips: "I got a little carried away
with this painting of a great
street in Philadelphia. It has an
abundance of texture in the
painting from spattering to my
original watercolor wash with
lots of pure white areas. The
watercolors benefit greatly by
having white spaces in them
to lighten the heaviness of the
pigments."

03. Title: *Mott Street General Store;*
Place: *New York, USA;* ***Duration:*** *1
week;* ***Size:*** *20 × 21 inches;* ***Tools &
Materials:*** *ink, pencil and watercolors*
The artist works quite a bit from
reference photos. A number
of years ago, he took a dozen
photos of the front of this building.
He taped them all together to
recreate the picture. From the
completed "stitched photos," he
did this painting. It changed the
way he works on his paintings
dramatically.

Tips: "This painting has
received a lot of attention as
it appeared in the Society of
Illustrator's Exhibition in New
York. The drawing was fairly
involved, so I could only work
for a few hours at a time. Once
the sketch was done, the inking
took several more days. I love
the painting part as it's fresh and
fairly quickly done."

Opporto, Portugal. At the top of the hill, overlooking the Duoro River.   Roger De Muth

04. *Title:* Overlooking the Duoro; *Place:* Opporto, Portugal; *Duration:* 6 days; *Size:* 20 × 14 inches; *Tools & Materials:* ink, pencil and watercolors

Opporto is an ancient Roman town built on cliffs overlooking the Duoro River. After a long steep walk, the artist chanced upon this ancient building on the way up to the top of the hill. You get a narrow glimpse of the buildings on the other side of the hill. It looks like it may have been a store at one time, with the wide folding doors. He loves visiting Portugal.

Tips: "I love the architecture in Opporto, so it was a pleasure to paint this building on a street overlooking the Duoro River. There are very light pastel paints in the distance on the painting, which almost look like bleached-out colors because of the dark facade on the house. The contrast makes the building more pronounced and brings it closer to the viewer."

05

Roger De Muth   120 Spring St. New York

05. Title: *120 Spring St;* **Place:** *New York, USA;* **Duration:** *4 hours;* **Size:** *6 × 6 inches;* **Tools & Materials:** *ink, pencil and watercolors*

This painting is a bit looser than the artist's other works, but it's more of a "sketch" painting. The Spring Street is an interesting place, and the shop in the center is called "Evolution." It's a mecca for dinosaur bones and natural science oddities. It looks good in the rain, too.

Tips: "This is a fairly loose sketch, followed by a loose painting. I love the reflection below the building on the water-washed street. The sketch took less than an hour because it's fairly small, the inking a couple of hours, and then the painting about an hour. I love quick paintings to balance the very involved paintings that take a week or more."

06. Title: *Buci News;* **Place:** *Paris, France;* **Duration:** *5 days;* **Size:** *15 × 10 inches;* **Tools & Materials:** *ink, pencil and watercolors*

The artist is having a show of his paintings at Syracuse University in November, and his part of the show will be paintings of "Stores, Storefronts, and Shop Keepers." This is one of his favorite shops in Paris. In fact, every shop in Paris is his favorite. He is looking forward to going back soon.

Tips: "This is a favorite painting, and a favorite place. Who doesn't love Paris? The painting is tight, but has loose qualities about it. I do a fair amount of spattering during the painting process with white to lighten the overall image. It gives the painting a fresher feel."

06

07   08

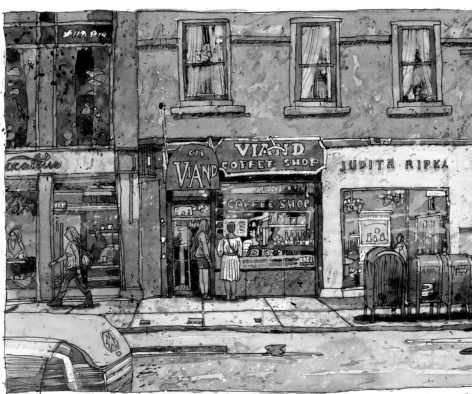

07. *Title:* The San Pio Hotel; *Place: Rome, Italy;* **Duration:** *3 days;* **Size:** *20 × 9 inches;* **Tools & Materials:** *ink, pencil and watercolors*

The San Pio Hotel is beautiful; Roger would go to Rome just to stay in the Hotel. The breakfast is wonderful, and it's near a landmark called the Keyhole. The view through the Keyhole is magnificent. You look through the most interesting formal garden and straight towards the Dome of St. Peter's Basilica. Ahh, Bella Roma.

Tips: "This is a fairly loose drawing mixed with a quick ink line. It's a view from the balcony in our hotel room in Aventino, Rome. I love the loose quality of the drawing and painting. To me, it's very fresh. I want to go back to Rome and do more paintings like this."

08. *Title:* The Viand Coffee Shop; *Place: New York, USA;* **Duration:** *6 days;* **Size:** *19 × 11 inches;* **Tools & Materials:** *ink, pencil and watercolors*

The Viand is one of the artist's favorite places to eat in New York. He's eaten there so often that the he's become friends with the owner, George Kontogiann. The artist has a number of his prints on display at the coffee shop. This painting was one of the first in his New York City Sketchbook, which he is working on now.

Tips: "I layer the paints from the lightest to the darkest colors. In the middle of the painting, I do a bit of spattering with Verditer and Holbein watercolor. It adds a bit of dimension to the painting, and more randomness. I finish with the darkest colors and use Payne's gray with burnt sienna mixed together. It creates a warm blue black color."

09. *Title:* Nantucket Winter St; *Place: Nantucket Island, USA;* **Duration:** *3 days;* **Size:** *15 × 12 inches;* **Tools & Materials:** *ink and watercolors*

The best part of vacations is getting lost. The artist loves it when he gets lost and finds himself near a place like this. This wonky house is on the Winter Street in Nantucket. It's not crooked like it is in his painting, but that's how it came out. He starts a sketch, and it keeps getting more and more out of line, then he looks at it and let go. Sometimes, letting go pays off.

Tips: "I call the style of this building 'wonky,' as it's all crooked. I start out with my usual sketch, but this time, it kept getting farther and farther distorted. It's one of my favorite paintings of Nantucket as it's so crooked and loose."

09

Lisbon, Portugal.

10. **Title:** *Lisbon Pleasure Trolley;* **Place:** *Lisbon, Portugal;* **Duration:** *4 days;* **Size:** *16 × 12 inches;* **Tools & Materials:** *ink, pencil and watercolors*

Lisbon is an incredible place, with marble sidewalks with different patterns in every neighborhood, historic stores that have't changed in a hundred years, and a great trolley line. When visiting a city like Lisbon, just hop on a trolley and see where it takes you. You'll be glad you did.

Tips: "I spent a couple of days drawing from my panorama photos for this scene. I shot perhaps a dozen photos, then stitched them together in Photoshop, and then transfered the drawing onto paper. Then I inked the drawing, let it dry and painted it. It took me a day or two to ink the drawing and about a day to paint it."

Mieke van der Merwe

Mieke van der Merwe graduated from the University of Stellenbosch in 2010 with a BA in Graphic Design. Afterward she worked in South Korea for two years, as an English teacher and freelance artist. She is currently busy with her Master's Degree in Children's Book Illustration at the University of Stellenbosch.

IN MY DRAWINGS I TRIED TO CAPTURE THAT BUSYNESS AND ALMOST A FEELING OF BEING OVERWHELMED BY ALL THE THINGS HAPPENING VISUALLY AT THE SAME TIME.

🧰 Mieke van der Merwe's drawing tools and materials

When drawing in my sketchbook or making work for exhibitions I like to work with pens, pencils, Japanese ink brush pens, watercolors and gouache. The one drawing tool I can't live without is my set of Rotring technical pens. The pens were introduced to me by my drawing lecturer at university and I have never used any other pens to do my fine ink drawings. What I particularly like about the pens are the thin stainless steel nibs that come in different line widths.

✒ Tools and materials recommended by Mieke van der Merwe

- 0.25 Rapidograph technical pen: This enables the artist to create detailed works with very fine lines using pens with 0.25 or 0.18 nibs or thicker lines for more expressive pieces with 0.35 or 0.5 nibs. The pens use ink cartridges which create excellent flowing lines that give work almost an etch or print-like feel.
- Pentel Aquash Waterbrush: This brushpen is a synthetic brush attached by a non-return valve to a hollow body which can be filled with ink. The harder you squeeze the pen the more ink it lets out to create thicker lines. The pen can also be filled with water which is ideal for blending watercolor pencils or applying watercolor, gouache or ink.
- Pocketsize watercolor set: Winsor & Newton has a wonderful watercolor set called Cotman Sketchers' Pocket Box, which comes with 12 different watercolors and an integral mixing pallet which makes it very easy to use wherever you go.
- Gouache paint: Winsor & Newton's Designer Gouache, as unlike other cheaper brands their paint last for years. The paint

also has a smooth even flow, and it glides across the paper, resulting in a flat, non-streaky finish. The colors are vibrant because of the high pigment concentration in the paint.

👁 City in my eyes

From 2011 to 2013 I stayed in South Korea and worked as an English teacher. The crowded cityscape was totally different from South Africa. This new space of visual chaos really stimulated me creatively. I especially loved sketching busy parts of Seoul, particularly Hongdae. In my drawings I tried to capture that busyness and almost a feeling of being overwhelmed by all the things happening visually at the same time.

01. *Title:* Iceskating in Paris; *Place:* Paris, France; *Duration:* 3 hours; *Size:* 42 × 59.4 cm; *Tools & Materials:* Japanese calligraphy brush pen

This work was created for a solo exhibition held at Gallery H, Ulsan, South Korea, titled "A Traveler's Perspective." When drawing the work the artist was fascinated by the windows and really enjoyed drawing the detail in them. The artist also tried to create a contrast by drawing the human figures actively ice-skating in the foreground against the detailed architectural background.

Tips: "For this work I first drew the basic outlines of the figures and architecture using a pencil. Thereafter I used a black ink brush pen to draw the work. The key is to have variation in line thickness when drawing the objects to give a more organic and lively feel to the work."

02. *Title: The Big Apple; Place: New York, USA; Duration: 3 hours; Size: 59.4 × 84.1 cm; Tools & Materials: Rotring radiograph 0.2mm technical pen, ink and brush*

This work was created for a group exhibition titled "One in a Million." The artist tried to create a piece which was visually intriguing and intricate to fit within the theme. New York can also be seen as a "one in a million city" because there is no other like it in the world.

Tips: "For this work I used a fine technical pen to draw the lines and patterns within the buildings. First I planned out the drawing working from a photograph whereafter I drew with pen on the rough pencil sketches. Try not to press too hard when drawing in pencil because it will be difficult to erase and spoil the picture."

03. *Title: Out of the Forest Came a City; Place: New York, USA; Duration: 3 hours; Size: 14 × 14 cm; Tools & Materials: Rotring radiograph 0.2 mm technical pen*

This work was created for a group exhibition titled "Let Yourself Love A Wild Thing," inspired by a quote, "If you go down to the woods today, you're sure of a big surprise." This made the artist think of how people used to demolish spaces to make way for cities and used it as the concept for this work. The title of the work "Out of the Forest Came A City" also demonstrates how the city has become the modern day forest seen as a concrete jungle.

Tips: "When drawing this picture I used different patterns on the buildings to create tonal value and areas of solid black to create contrast. By doing so it creates the illusion of depth within the work."

03

Out of the forest came a city

Mieke van der Merwe

04. Title: *Johannesburg Skyline;* **Place:** *Johannesburg, South Africa;* **Duration:** *3 hours;* **Size:** *59.4 x 59.4 cm;* **Tools & Materials:** *Rotring radiograph 0.2 mm technical pen, ink and brush*

"Home is Where I Am with You" is a group exhibition supporting an orphanage located in the Cape Town townships. Most of the works depict places the artists have traveled to or have sentimental value towards. This work is of Johannesburg, also known as Jozi, Joburg, Joni, eGoli or Joeys, abbreviated as JHB, the largest city in South Africa, by population. Johannesburg is the provincial capital of Gauteng, the wealthiest province in South Africa. It has the largest economy among the metropolitan regions in Sub-Saharan Africa.

Tips: "For this work I worked from a photograph that had a light coming in from the one side, casting shadows on the buildings behind them. Drawing from such a photo it makes it easier to create contrast in the work, especially if I'm working in black and white."

05. *Title:* *The Old Biscuit Mill;* *Place:* *Woodstock, South Africa;* *Duration:* *3 hours;* *Size:* *29.7 × 21 cm;* *Tools & Materials:* *gouache, ink and brush*

This work illustrates the old biscuit mill at a vibrant, warmhearted little village in the heart of Woodstock, where talented people come together to share and collaborate. The Mill is home to day and night markets, dynamic office space, a range of workshops and designer stores, delicious farm stalls, and decadent restaurants as well as an inspiring line-up of festivals and productions. Every Saturday there is an organic market that attracts many locals and tourists.

Tips: "In this work I started by drawing the picture with an ink brush on paper. Then I painted on the ink drawing with gouache and touched it up with ink on top of the paint after it dried."

06. *Title:* *Fisheye;* *Place:* *Hong Kong, China;* *Duration:* *3 hours;* *Size:* *59.4 × 84.1 cm;* *Tools & Materials:* *Rotring radiograph 0.2 mm technical pen, ink and brush*

This work was created for a group show titled "The Editions Show." The exhibition is consisted of a collection of printed media works by contemporary artists located in Cape Town. The artist's work for this show was inspired by her mum's vintage camera collection and the world through the camera viewfinder. This work is of Hong Kong drawn from a photograph taken with a fish-eye camera.

Tips: "This work was first drawn with a pen on paper whereafter I scanned it in on the computer and edited it in Photoshop. In Photoshop it was then colored in using a Bamboo tablet which allows me to press harder or softer to create a more natural and realistic painting effect."

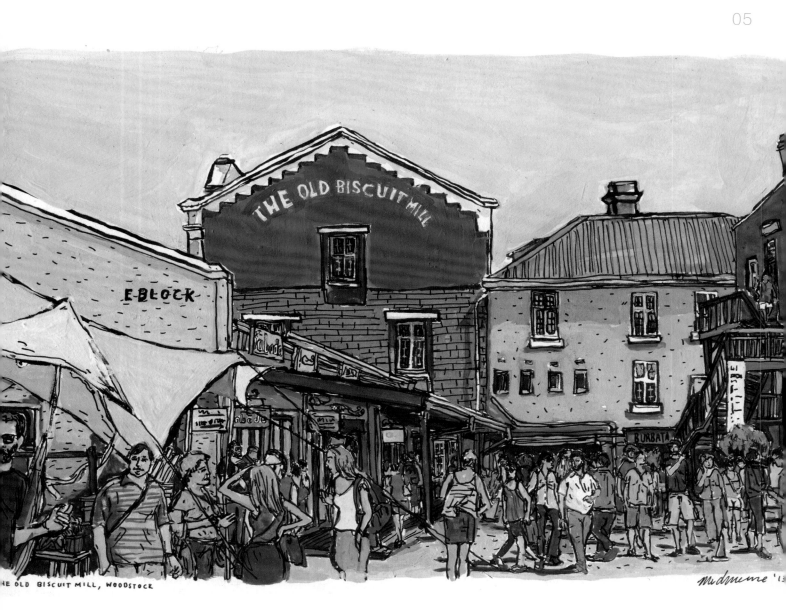

THE OLD BISCUIT MILL, WOODSTOCK

07. *Title: Graaff-Reinet Church; Place: Graaff-Reneit, South Africa; Duration: 3 hours; Size: 21 × 29.7 cm; Tools & Materials: gouache, ink and brush*

This work depicts the church in the city centre of Graaff-Reinet. Graaff-Reinet was established in 1786 and is the fourth oldest town in South Africa and the oldest town in Eastern Cape Province. It was established to bring law & order, religion and education to the many Dutch farmers on the Eastern Frontier. The town is renowned for its architectural heritage, and at 220 sites has more national monuments than any other town in South Africa. It is a popular tourist attraction and is well known for its beautiful church made from locally made bricks.

Tips: "For this work I used a good quality watercolor paper. The work was first drawn on the paper with pen and painted with watercolor afterwards. I kept some areas white to keep the work fresh and not to overdo the color."

08. *Title: Venice; Place: Venice, Italy; Duration: 3 hours; Size: 19 × 25 cm; Tools & Materials: Moleskine journal, Rotring radiograph 0.2 mm technical pen, watercolor*

In 2009 the artist went on a European tour where she made a travel journal of the cities she visited. During her 3-week stay she collected cards, cash slips and train tickets and drew her new surroundings. When she visited Venice the romantic aura around the canals and gondolas fascinated her, which inspired her to make his work. By adding the watercolor to the picture the artist tried to capture something of the atmosphere she felt during her stay.

Tips: "For this work I drew first and applied the watercolor afterwards. When I applied the watercolor I mixed the colors with browns and yellows to give the work more of a romantic dreamy feel."

08

09. *Title:* City Hall; *Place:* Cape Town, South Africa; *Duration:* 3 hours; *Size:* 29.7 × 21 cm; *Tools & Materials:* Rotring radiograph 0.2 mm technical pen, ink and brush

This drawing of the City Hall in Cape Town illustrates the beautiful British architecture of one of the oldest buildings in the city. Built in 1905, It is a very well-known location in Cape Town, as it is where Nelson Mandela made his first speech in 1990 after he was released from prison.

Tips: "In this work I worked with black and white using pen and ink. Some of the buildings are drawn a bit crooked and skewed, which contributes to the handmade and organic feel of the work."

10. *Title:* Streets of Venice; *Place:* Venice, Italy; *Duration:* 3 hours; *Size:* 42 × 59.4 cm; *Tools & Materials:* Japanese calligraphy brush pen

This work depicts the streets of Venice during twilight and how the shadows become longer and fall onto the water. Using the thick black ink lines creates a contrast with the negative white spaces. The work creates a feeling of a lazy afternoon strolling along the canals.

Tips: "I used flat areas of solid black to suggest shadows in this work. This creates a contrast in the work and makes it look more dramatic and bold."

10

11. *Title:* Purple Turtle; *Place:* Cape Town, South Africa; *Duration:* 3 hours; *Size:* 17.5 × 21 cm; *Tools & Materials: Rotring radiograph 0.2 mm technical pen, and watercolor*

This building in the Long Street in Cape Town is called the Purple Turtle and is well known for its bright purple color and friendly regulars. Long Street, where this building is located, is a major street in the City Bowl section of Cape Town. It is famous as a bohemian hangout and the street is lined with many bookstores, various ethnic restaurants and bars. The Long Street has many buildings with Victorian follies and intricate ironwork, which have been mostly well kept.

Tips: "In this work I first drew the building with pen and painted it in with watercolor afterwards. The watercolor is also applied in a very loose and expressive manner giving the work a personalised feel."

12. *Title:* A Street View in Paris; *Place:* Paris, France; *Duration:* 3 hours; *Size:* 29.7 × 42 cm; *Tools & Materials: Rotring radiograph 0.2 mm technical pen, ink and brush*

This piece depicts the streets of Paris and the intricate rooftops of the city skyline. In this work the artist played around with different patterns and textures using line to give dimension to the work. The perspective of this work is like having a bird's eye view, exploring the city as if you were flying over it.

Tips: "While creating this work, I used Rotring pens of different hib widths for thinner and thicker line work. I then combined this with an ink brush pen to fill in the black areas."

11

12

Choo Meng Foo

Meng Foo is a man with many interests. He paints, writes and designs. He is trained in arts, architecture, and urban design, and graduated from the National University of Singapore with a Bachelor in Arts, Bachelor in Architecture and Master in Urban Studies. For him, life is about learning and experiencing the myriad possibilities that society and nature offers. Art is life and living is creating art. He works with acrylic, watercolor, ink and photography. His works had been exhibited in museums, universities, and galleries. His works have been featured in *Asian Geographic*, *DK*, *Wave*, *One* and *Silverlining*. His art works are collected locally and overseas.

🧰 Choo Meng Foo's drawing tools and materials

My tools are a camera, stitching softwares and a good pair of boots for walking with ample time to soak myself in the place. I use the fountain pen to create my line drawings on a sketch pad and then scan them into the computer to add the colors. Output is done on archival artist paper using professional Epson printers.

🖌 Tools and materials recommended by Choo Meng Foo

- Fuji X100: A neat little camera that helps to capture the scene with good contrast and details.
- Fountain Pen: 1911 standard Sailor fountain pen with the EF nibs. They produce consistent thin beautiful lines.
- Sketch Pad: Fabrino Schizzi Chlorine and acid free cellulose paper pad 90 grams. I like its smoothness and it keeps the ink intact and does not spread, resulting in very thin lines.
- Photoshop: Software application that allows me to trace the lines digitally and color them. The application is easy to use and versatile.
- ICE: A free software application by Microsoft which helps to stitch the photographs much better than other applications.

👁 City in my eyes

Singapore is a green and clean city with a population of about five million. It is well known for its sustainable city planning, with work, leisure and learning integrated into every aspect of the urban fabric. People are friendly and the crime rate is one of the lowest in the world. Order and efficiency is what comes to the mind of every visitor to the country.

> " ART IS THAT FREEDOM WHERE THE BRUSH WRITES THE MIND INSTANTLY AND PERFECTLY! "

Photography: Choo Meng Foo

01

01. *Title:* I am unique; *Place:* Tiong Bahru, Singapore; *Duration:* 3 hours; *Size:* 21 × 14.8 cm; *Tools & Materials:* Sailor fountain pen, Pelikan ink on paper, scanned, digitally colored and digitally printed on archival paper
This is a unique building designed in the art deco style which imitates the streamline of steam ships and air planes. It defines housing as a "Machine for living."

Tips: "What is here may not be around in a few years, so cherish them while we can."

02

03

02. *Title:* *Debt Hotline 6844 0221 – GBA 3365Z;* *Place:* *Tiong Bahru, Singapore;* *Duration:* *3 hours;* *Size:* *21 × 14.8 cm;* *Tools & Materials:* *Sailor fountain pen, Pelikan ink on paper, scanned, digitally colored and digitally printed on archival paper*
Debt collecting becomes a real profession and it made its appearance in Tiong Bahru. This marked a certain period in this urban landscape.

Tips: "Time changes, people change, places change, habit changes, and God is in the detail."

03. *Title:* *Tiong Bahru Fairy Tales;* *Place:* *Tiong Bahru, Singapore;* *Duration:* *3 hours;* *Size:* *21 × 14.8 cm;* *Tools & Materials:* *Sailor fountain pen, Pelikan ink on paper, scanned, digitally colored and digitally printed on archival paper*
There aren't many places in Singapore that have this architectural feature in the back lane. Also interesting is that the handles that were attached to the right of every back door. It is puzzling.

Tips: "Look out for the differences, where the gap can pry open an entire world."

04. *Title:* Sin Hoi Sai Sea Food Restaurant; *Place:* Tiong Bahru, Singapore; *Duration:* 3 hours; *Size:* 21 × 14.8 cm; *Tools & Materials:* Sailor fountain pen, Pelikan ink on paper, scanned, digitally colored and digitally printed on archival paper

This is one of the famous Chinese restaurants in Tiong Bahru, and many people came from afar to taste the good food. It is well known for the most expensive Alaskan crab, which costs $700 a plate. It has become notorious, and has marked the memories of the good old days when it did not cost that much.

Tips: "Mix the age-old fountain pen and the latest technology, and marry them into a single possibility."

05. *Title:* No Ordinary Bean Curd; *Place:* Tiong Bahru, Singapore; *Duration:* 3 hours; *Size:* 21 × 14.8 cm; *Tools & Materials:* Sailor fountain pen, Pelikan ink on paper, scanned, digitally colored and digitally printed on archival paper

Here people see Chinese characters catering to the Chinese community that is building up among the residents of Tiong Bahru. It indicates the shift towards adopting the Chinese lingo in the choice of words, signifying a shift in the attitudes towards inclusion of Chinese influence.

Tips: "Look out for uniqueness or changes in the environment; never stop observing and recording."

05

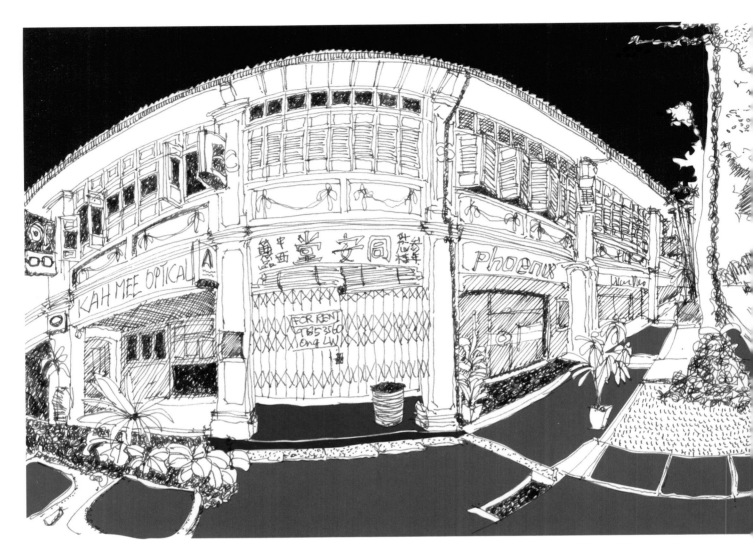

06

06. *Title:* Tong An Tang Chinese Pharmacy; *Place:* Tiong Bahru, Singapore; *Duration:* 3 hours; *Size:* 21 × 14.8 cm; *Tools & Materials:* Sailor fountain pen, Pelikan ink on paper, scanned, digitally colored and digitally printed on archival paper
The Chinese pharmacy has folded up and the unit is for rent. Perhaps the owners of the pharmacy had not moved with times or perhaps they were too old to carry on the business and their children were not continuing the business, signifying a certain era had passed.

Tips: "Change is timeless. Keep learning, experimenting and create varieties."

07. *Title:* Big Mama; *Place:* Tiong Bahru, Singapore; *Duration:* 3 hours; *Size:* 21 × 14.8 cm; *Tools & Materials:* Sailor fountain pen, Pelikan ink on paper, scanned, digitally colored and digitally printed on archival paper
The old good Mama cooking reminds us of home-cooked food, and perhaps brings us some good old memories of this place.

Tips: "Straight lines become curves to give us much wider angles, so that we can see the complete building in close proximity."

07

SKETCH CITY: Tips and Inspiration for Drawing on Location
Author: Dopress Books
Commissioning Editors: Guo Guang, Mang Yu, Yvonne Zhao, Chen Hao
English Editors: Jenny Qiu, Vera Pan
Copy Editor: Frances Moxley Zinder
Book Designer: Peng Tao

First published in the United Kingdom in 2015 by CYPI PRESS

Add: 79 College Road, Harrow Middlesex, HA1 1BD, UK
Tel: +44 (0) 20 3178 7279
E-mail: sales@cypi.net editor@cypi.net
Website: www.cypi.co.uk
ISBN: 978-1-908175-64-9
Printed in China